LARA VAN ZUYDAM

A
MODERN
GUIDE TO EVOLVING
IN A CONSCIOUS
UNIVERSE

REDFeather™
MIND | BODY | SPIRIT

Designed by BMac
Cover design by BMac
Cover photo credit: Shutterstock | McLura
Type set in Minion Pro/ New Frank

ISBN: 978-0-7643-6767-0
Printed in India

Published by REDFeather Mind, Body, Spirit
An imprint of Schiffer Publishing, Ltd.
4880 Lower Valley Road
Atglen, PA 19310
Phone: (610) 593-1777; Fax: (610) 593-2002
Email: Info@redfeathermbs.com
Web: www.redfeathermbs.com

For our complete selection of fine books on this and related subjects, please visit our website at www.redfeathermbs.com. You may also write for a free catalog.

REDFeather Mind, Body, Spirit's titles are available at special discounts for bulk purchases for sales promotions or premiums. Special editions, including personalized covers, corporate imprints, and excerpts, can be created in large quantities for special needs. For more information, contact the publisher.

We are always looking for people to write books on new and related subjects. If you have an idea for a book, please contact us at proposals@schifferbooks.com.

FSC
www.fsc.org
MIX
Paper from
responsible sources
FSC® C016779

CONTENTS

ACKNOWLEDGMENTS

F oremost, I offer heartfelt thanks to my husband, Jason van Zuydam, who has acted as a sounding board throughout the process of bringing this book to life, offering his ever-practical advice and moral support.

I would also like to express my deep gratitude to Severine Jeauneau, my inspiring agent, who noticed that I had a book to write and worked patiently with me to bring it to fruition, fielding my various questions with so much grace. Thank you to Kim Arnold for graciously inviting me to speak at her UK Tarot Conference in 2021—an event at which I was fated to meet Severine.

I also offer my sincere thanks to my editor, Peggy Kellar, as well as to Brenda McCallum, my cover and interior designer, for tuning into the essence of this book so ably, and for their keen foresight.

Thank you to my dear friends Richard Abbot and Javier Martinez for encouraging me to write. Richard inspired me to get practical about writing, and I distinctly recall how, about a decade ago, Javier persistently badgered me to pack in my day job and write spiritual fiction. It was a laughable idea to me at the time, and this book isn't fiction, but I think it counts.

Naturally, I also offer my thanks to the unseen beings who have influenced the publication of this book for the highest good, and to the members of my soul family who have offered me the experiences—both joyful and challenging—that I have needed to undergo in this lifetime (and will continue to undergo as long as I am in this dense physical body).

I AM NOT THIS BODY

I am not this body
With its flawed personality

The stiffness in my limbs
The resistance to moving on my mat
The injury that won't go away

I am not the aching
The crushing reminder that your love is conditional

I am not the knife edge of those words
flung around so carelessly
Little daggers into my heart

Telling me to do something practical when I wiped your brow
Taking back your hand when I tried to hold it
Calling my friend's mother to tell her that I would not be attending
That night when the flat next door burned down while
I slept fitfully in the passageway
When I fell over as you looked on
Unforgiving in the face of my mistakes

I am not these repeating patterns
But I am a collaborator

I am merely visiting here
This pain a necessary friction

PREFACE

When I was a child, I was aware of a consciousness that seemed to speak to me from within. It didn't speak in words; instead, it spoke in feelings. Instinctively, I knew that I must pay attention to it.

I had a vivid imagination as a child, playing out scenes in which I was a dancer, performing for a make-believe audience, imagining Little Red Riding Hood's wolf in the looming forests of the South African "Midlands Meander" as we drove past them. As my imagination expanded, my consciousness began to flow more strongly. Imagination is the breeding ground of delusion in its unbalanced state, but also the entryway to the mysteries.

Subtle information usually appeared in times of pain, when I felt a sense of loneliness and desolation, perplexed by how alien I felt in my environment or when I felt unloved, and I saw cruelty in the world. It appeared at the times when I had apparently reached rock bottom, and I knew that I had a binary choice: pull myself together or lose myself completely in the misery that I was feeling.

On those occasions, I knew that I had to turn inward and engage with something inside myself. I knew that I would survive the latest emotional upheaval. But I also knew that I had to do it on my own. You see, in my particular soul paradigm, I couldn't rely on others to help me out. That pattern was a necessary friction to encourage me to grow. As a child, I knew that I needed to cultivate a sense of fortitude and emotional self-reliance as I navigated my early years. This was a lesson that had followed me through many lifetimes.

The inner voice was determined, adamant, and persistent. It encouraged me to love myself. It also grounded me, helping me curb the flow of emotion that—unchecked—would have obstructed my spiritual growth.

My consciousness made itself apparent in other ways too. It seemed to have a very strong sense of what was and wasn't good for me. It encouraged me to speak my truth at critical times, nudging me to stand up in an assembly hall of two hundred disapproving teenaged girls, the sole dissenting voice in the face of mass complacency. It forced me to speak authentically. It was also innately resistant to any form of peer pressure. I found that I instinctively hated cigarettes, even in the early nineties, when people were still allowed to smoke in public places and before those disturbing images of diseased organs began to appear on cigarette packaging. I mostly eschewed alcohol in my university days, preferring to face the vicissitudes of late adolescence and my emerging sense of self in complete sobriety.

This story isn't intended to be a criticism of those who have made different choices—you see, years later I realized that my natal chart revealed quite plainly a classic tendency toward addiction. My instinctive aversion to things that could become addictive was important—it was a call to action in my best interests. Somehow, I had managed to steer clear of the things that would be harmful to my progress, and I must give credit to my invisible helpers for nudging me along a safer path.

It would be a while before I recognized this consciousness as my soul and that having a team of spiritual aides is every human being's birthright.

I am not suggesting that I had (or indeed have) all the answers or that I am somehow "special" because I have had certain experiences. On the contrary, everyone has their own story and their own unique challenges. I had to learn to balance my innate caution with a degree of adaptability. As a child and into my early adulthood, I was a chronic worrier with low self-esteem, and I was extremely rigid in my worldview. I wouldn't be told (which, to be fair, wasn't always a bad thing), and occasionally I made ridiculous choices. I needed to learn to filter what I communicated to others to ensure that it landed in the right way, and to develop compassion. I also had to learn that situations are rarely binary; it's the nuances, the more nebulous shades of gray, that contribute to the path of wisdom.

For as long as I can remember, I have been drawn to spirituality; this natural gravitation at a certain point in an incarnation toward something higher is part of what the second-century Hindu sage Patanjali was referring to when he expounded upon the practice of yoga (which comes from the word "union" in Sanskrit).

When my family visited my maternal grandparents in the coastal town of Durban, I would always make a beeline for my grandfather's book on "unexplained mysteries." I sensed that mystery was all around me.

It wasn't, therefore, surprising that I had a brief encounter with organized religion as a teenager—that is, until my inner sense of self-determination asserted itself, and I could no longer ignore the moral fascism that I felt prevailed in that particular community, and the weakness and dependency that it engendered among many of its targets. I was young and fairly naive, but keenly aware of the need to know for myself what I considered to be "right" and "wrong." I wasn't going to be told that premarital sex, karate, and reflexology were somehow "evil." It wasn't long before I distanced myself from that community and its misguided attempts to deny all "evil," and began to indulge my fascination with the occult—another word for "unknown."

As I turned my attention to developing my psychic faculties, initially by way of an intense interest (appearing out of nowhere) in occult literature and crystals, I began to become aware of the existence of a finer energetic body that coexisted with my dense physical body, linking me to subtler dimensions.

This energetic body first made itself apparent during a tai chi retreat near the medieval city of Urbino in Italy. The venue was a delight to the senses—an endless view of the Italian countryside and an attic bedroom that was accessible only by ladder.

As I flowed through the tai chi forms in a dome-shaped room overlooking the hills, moving an invisible ball of energy (or "chi") around my body, I suddenly became viscerally aware of a strong pulling sensation at the top of my head as my crown chakra, the seventh energy center in the system of etheric wheels in the human body, was activated.

Years later, I recognized this event as the burning away of the etheric web that protected my crown chakra by the "fire of mind," blended with the two fires of matter (kundalini and pranic fire), allowing for an effective conduit for the downflow of higher information. I discuss these technical terms in detail in chapter 1.

Later on in the tai chi retreat, I had my first tangible contact with the beings that I will interchangeably refer to as "guides," "spirit guides," and "guardian angels." It was an odd experience: I wasn't participating in a guided meditation; I was merely sitting in a meditative state, cross-legged in that dome in the Italian countryside, free of any mind-altering substances, yet situated on top of a vast mountain. My contact with those beings was spontaneous—they simply appeared, apparently of their own volition. I hadn't called them—I was simply surveying the inner landscape on top of that etheric mountain, without any expectations. To my intensely analytical mind, that gave the experience a significant amount of credibility.

The tai chi retreat was a catalyst for a period of significant spiritual growth over a period of approximately seven years in which I immersed myself in Tarot and Western and Eastern mysticism. I also began to explore astrology, and I learned about the risks associated with working with beings on other planes—I cover some of those risks in chapter 4. Thus began my (initially unconscious) work to liberate myself from the endless cycle of birth and rebirth as a soul incarnating on Earth.

During those important years, I remained ignorant of the conceptual differences in some of the esoteric jargon that I was encountering. In particular, I wasn't sure where to draw the line between such notions as "soul," "spirit," "higher self," and "Holy Guardian Angel." At that time, I vaguely sensed the differences, and I was in active communication with other beings, but I wasn't fully aware that I had a soul that was in the process of reincarnating over and over again as a human being.

Later, I noticed that apparently none of the preeminent modern and premodern authors of spirituality and mysticism had properly attempted to define these terms. They tended to be evasive on the distinctions between certain definitions—or at least vague or speculative, rarely offering credible definitions. More frustratingly, their teachings would assume that the reader understood what they meant by "soul." It seemed ironic that they were offering beginner-level spiritual content to an audience who they assumed to be well versed in the vastly more complex notion of the soul.

Some authors in the field of spirituality and mysticism avoid the concept of soul altogether, relegating the process of spiritual evolution to external (or form-based) factors rather than to internal (or spirit-based) factors—a tendency that is counterintuitive to the spiritual progress, and the consequences of which are extremely severe, as I outline in chapter 8.

Without exception, my early astrology teachers consciously avoided dealing with the tricky question of the soul in chart readings—in some cases while they taught the works of Plato and other ancient luminaries in this area. Temporarily chastened by uncomfortable silences and brusque references to the school's house rules, I quickly learned to suppress any commentary that I had on chart interpretations from a soul perspective—at least until I began to practice as an astrologer in my own right.

Some of my teachers seemed to be distinctly uncomfortable with the idea that they might house an immortal being that they didn't have the appropriate mental equipment to comprehend, and in respect of which they apparently had limited control. They were horrified that a soul might choose to incarnate as a starving child or with some terrible physical affliction—or into a family rife with abuse. One teacher put forward an argument that reincarnation was fundamentally discriminatory and, therefore, anathema as a philosophical framework. My answer to that is "Yes, it is discriminatory, but every soul must go through the range of experiences." That doesn't mean that we should abdicate responsibility for difficult socioeconomic circumstances—it simply means that we should not engage in unnecessary self-flagellation during the course of our lives for not being born into more challenging circumstances and self-sabotage to such an extent that we are unable to carry out the work that we need to undertake in the current lifetime to be effective as a soul.

While some astrology teachers include the work of the ancients on the soul in their teachings, they make it their primary business to attempt to discredit reincarnation (which I discuss in the next chapter), leaving organized religion relatively unscathed. Of course, the astrologers among you know that some astrologers choose to relegate astrology to an exclusively psychological paradigm, which they are quite entitled to do. But we also know that in some quarters, fear leads to the active suppression of truth. I want to encourage an approach to teaching and learning in which all modalities are embraced as possibilities, and it is left open to the student to choose their preferred philosophy, free of judgment.

I have singled out astrology teachers since in all my occult studies, the area of astrology is the only system of divination in which there is an active intention on the part of many practitioners to stamp out a soul-based approach to interpretation. It seems that in their attempts to hang on to a modicum of empirical respectability (even though astrology very clearly transcends modern science), some individuals are determined not to look under any stones in case they accidentally uncover something unpalatable to them. This is particularly egregious where other spiritual lives are potentially in their hands.

I suppose the point that I really want to make is that this book has been born of a need not only to share what I have learned about the human soul and how it manifests itself, but also how best to leverage the experience that each of us is born with. One of the central aims of this book is to help readers begin to think practically about what to do with the knowledge that human beings have souls and that our souls are intricately woven into a much larger system, inhabited, by the way, by other beings: *Yes, I can sense that I have a soul. Now what do I do with that knowledge? What are the consequences and risks of not doing anything with that knowledge?*

This book aims to bring awareness to the reader and to focus the mind by demystifying the notion of "soul." It lays out the markers and explains what human beings all have to work with, on the basis of their individual blueprints. Think of it as a productivity manual of sorts for getting the best out of your particular experience in this lifetime. It won't vanquish your pain or your grief or your loss, past, present, or future. But I hope it *will* help you make more sense of why your life is such a mixed bag of elation and sadness. Importantly, it will help you steer that precarious course with equanimity, so that when the tough times come (and they will come), you have the tools necessary to navigate the course.

As I foreshadowed above, I also wanted to offer what has been conspicuously lacking in occult texts for a very, very long time: a granular explanation of the concept of "soul" and how the soul fits into the broader cosmic ecosystem.

INTRODUCTION

Shortly before I knew that I would be delivering a presentation on Alice A. Bailey's *Esoteric Astrology*[1] as part of the OPA's[2] UK panel event in 2021, I had an unusual dream. I was a diver submerged in an unknown sea. There was a strange, green light all around me in the water, and I could scarcely see ahead for all the verdant oppression.

I should tell you that I have never dived in my waking life, unless you count the frequent deep dives into the icy waters that Neptune governs in my natal birth chart. Or perhaps with some poetic license (and for maximum drama) we can include all those times that I drowned in my past lives, as well as one in which I was tasked with the ordeal of retrieving an assortment of implements from beneath the waters as a fledgling "medicine man." Those incidents might account for my obstinate refusal as a six-year-old to put my head under water.

Yet, there I was, forensically cleaning the grimy bow of a gargantuan ship. I was aware of the inherent dangers of my task, yet oddly unafraid. The ship was dark and old, brooding in the waters. It was waiting to embark on an enigmatic voyage. Precisely where it was going was not for me to know, but I did know that the direction was forward.

Months later, I was a somnambulant visitor once more, this time to a primordial landscape, in the center of which was an abyss. I was being shown humanity's positioning relative to this chasm—a cosmic tunnel, an interchange so astonishing that I do not have the words to effectively describe it. Once again, I sensed danger, and I was aware of my insignificance in this place. On the other hand, I knew that I was being tasked with uncovering some of its mysteries.

So began my efforts to bring fully to human consciousness one of our greater mysteries, the soul, within its wider frame of reference or operating system, removing the dross that has accumulated through the ages to confuse and obfuscate as humanity has reinvented itself over and over again; to bring the information to the cold light of the twenty-first-century day.

I hope to do things differently in this book, as is fitting in modern times, so that readers might deliberately apply what they see here toward self-improvement—self-improvement that surpasses the limitations of mere personality. Self-improvement that goes much, much deeper.

In my efforts to elucidate the concept of the human soul, I have referred to the works of some other authors who have written on the subject (to varying degrees of abstruseness); in particular, I have referred to the revelatory works of nineteenth-century mystic Alice A. Bailey, who was born in England and spent most of her life in the United States. When she was eventually pushed to expose the source of her work, she reluctantly revealed that it was mostly channeled from a being who referred to himself interchangeably as "the Tibetan" or the master Djwal Khul. Alice's books typically contain an extract from a statement by the Tibetan, in which he explains that he lives in a physical body "on the borders of Tibet" and that he occasionally, "from the exoteric standpoint," supervises "a large group of Tibetan lamas." In this statement, highlighting the overriding need for discernment, he wisely says:

> *The books that I have written are sent out with no claim for their acceptance. They may, or may not, be correct, true, and useful. It is for you to ascertain their truth by right practice and by the exercise of the intuition. Neither I nor A.A.B. is the least interested in having them acclaimed as inspired writings, or in having anyone speak of them (with bated breath) as being the work of one of the Masters. If they present truth in such a way that it follows sequentially upon that already offered in the world teachings, if the information given raises the aspiration and the will-to-serve from the plane of the emotions to that of the mind (the plane whereon the Masters can be found), then they will have served their purpose. If the teaching conveyed calls forth a response from the illumined mind of the worker in the world and brings a flashing forth of his intuition, then let that teaching be accepted. But not otherwise. If the statements meet with eventual corroboration or are deemed true under the test of the Law of Correspondences, then that is well and good. But should this not be so, let not the student accept what is said.*
>
> *...*

Much could be speculated about the Tibetan and the fact that Alice says she channeled information from him. It is particularly fascinating that he says he was alive in physical form when he transmitted the information to Alice—it is as possible that he was a contemporary of Alice's in a different geographical location as it is possible that he existed in physical form, but in a different timeline.

Right off the bat, I must credit much of the detailed technical content of this book to Alice and her unseen instructor. Her work is largely unknown other than in small esoteric circles with a mystical leaning. I have spent countless hours reviewing Alice's writings and piecing together important threads of esoteric knowledge so that I could weave it into a coherent whole. I should mention that what I present in this book is merely the tip of the proverbial iceberg—there is far more to be unpacked.

When I first discovered Alice, I quickly realized that she was able to offer the more granular information that underpins the wider esoteric framework that I had come to understand. I had craved these missing details, and then, suddenly, they had presented themselves to me in the form of a set of almost nondescript indigo-blue books whose contents told the story of the cosmos. Yet, I was still a little skeptical. For a while, like any diligent lawyer, I tested references to mind-bogglingly abstract concepts in one book against similar references in another, testing for inconsistencies that might undermine the credibility of their contents (and perhaps confirm that it was all just a dazzlingly complex esoteric hoax). Yet, the contents withstood my testing. They were remarkably consistent, and I finally judged that I could trust the source.

Alice often comments on and develops the work of Helena Blavatsky, a Russian mystic also born in the nineteenth century, whose religious system of Theosophy has variously been embraced or criticized over the past century or so. I have occasionally quoted Blavatsky in this book; I was interested to find as I reviewed her writings that I was sometimes critical of Blavatsky's positioning of some esoteric content—mostly because it occasionally comes across as an admonition and too exacting in areas. And that's exactly the point: I am always keen to bring out the nuances of esoteric information and to give reasons for why I say things rather than purporting to dictate how my audience chooses to respond to that information. The audience of the twenty-first century is often of a higher energetic constitution and does not necessarily take kindly to being told what to do. Unfortunately, that finer vibration also makes it far easier for twenty-first-century humanity to give life to destructive creations on a mass scale, such as violence, fear, and greed, and then to fall victim to those creations on the basis of group "think."

Having said all of that, a reference to a particular author's work in this book should not necessarily be misconstrued as my universal acceptance of that author's ideology. As is typical of my style, which is to avoid throwing the baby out with the bath water, I draw upon elements that are useful to me, and ignore what is not useful, having consciously subjected my own belief system to rigorous challenge and scrutiny. "Belief" system is perhaps not the right word; "my reality" is probably more accurate.

Like many other authors and philosophers before me, some of my work might be said to be derivative of those thinkers who have previously tried to articulate this behemoth of an abstraction. I make no apology for that since the driving force behind my own work is not originality (I make no claims to groundbreaking discoveries); instead, it is clarity and, in part, resurrection of bodies of work that have long remained dormant. Polishing up a tarnished piece of antique jewelry to reveal its original beauty—or perhaps scraping the barnacles off the bow of a ship so that it is not impeded in its journey.

That said, I do not consider myself to be a philosopher, nor have I undertaken a critical analysis of existing philosophical works. It is not my intention to deconstruct possible inconsistencies and linguistic ambiguities in Plato's works, for example, or to call out flaws in some of the views of individual authorities or in the outmoded ideologies of some of the societies from which they drew their inspiration. Rather, it is the responsibility of each and every reader to make their own judgments, responsibly and with integrity, weighing all the relevant factors to form an accurate picture—deliberately penetrating the shadows, the things that make us uncomfortable.

We humans are a strange mix of light and dark; this is hardwired into us from birth when we first enter the stage. Grappling with that dichotomy is a lifelong struggle for each and every individual. It is a mistake, therefore, to unthinkingly contribute to the growing "cancel culture" in society if we see or hear something that triggers us or incites fear. We must bravely undergo the friction of challenge to become stronger. If we constantly avoid the friction, the result is inevitably a lack of resilience and subsequent weakness. Bear with me as I flesh out this theme later in the book.

I recently attended a fascinating astrology talk on reading the probability of death from an astrological chart. It was a small, intimate gathering of astrologers, and we all knew that there are very few circumstances indeed in which reading someone's death from a chart is appropriate, but that we astrologers need to have the tools to carry out that analysis where that type of service is needed. Presenting numerous cases in which a range of astrologers had successfully predicted the timing and nature of death, the speaker wisely counseled the group against quashing the use of these tools (or avoiding the subject of death because it is "triggering") to such an extent that the methods become otiose and fade into obscurity, making it impossible for astrologers to do the service work that they have made available in societies for thousands of years—from Baghdad to Birmingham. Much like lawyers, astrologers must be strictly impartial—they must not judge a client's conduct in a case; instead, they must simply point out the possibilities. I talk about the subject of death in more detail in chapter 2.

What I am hoping to present in this book is a coherent picture from my own point of view, drawing on other authors' theories where it is constructive to do so, of a most abstract topic. Abstract because, in part, no one seems to have taken the time to properly unpack the notion of "soul," with the result that it tends to be dimly understood and often used interchangeably with "spirit," sometimes correctly and at other times ignorantly. Where others have asserted factual abstractions relating to the soul as the basic foundation for still-more-esoteric teachings, I have tried to go back to the basics of what I consider to be the "technology" of soul.

In addition, I hope to be able to demonstrate how that picture can be used to support day-to-day life as a twenty-first-century human. I hope that by the twenty-second century, the majority of humanity will have significantly moved forward in its evolution as a group, even if the frictions around them have only increased.

In the main, we tend to abuse the term "soul"; we use it irresponsibly for concepts that we seem to have very little real understanding of. If we can sense the latent power inherent in the notion of "soul," its mystery, and its importance, why aren't we making it our business to reach for a better understanding? Our own ignorance makes us uncomfortable. The literate among us, and the wise, gloss over the abstraction; we relegate it to poetry and to "passion"—perhaps the same passion that drives us to do unspeakable things. We talk about "heart and soul," but what do we really mean? Either we must drive it out of our vocabulary for lack of meaning or embrace it fully in all its light: the light of illumination, the light of growth.

The subject of the soul and its cosmic ecosystem may be one with which you are profoundly familiar, but perhaps like me, you are striving to understand the mechanics at a more granular level, the main objective (apart from burning curiosity) being to maximize growth in the current lifetime.

Perhaps you are a curious bystander or a cynic, in which case I would respectfully remind you that modern science, much like the Catholic Church in Galileo's time, suffers from a lack of awareness of the risk of falling victim to unknown unknowns, dismissing anything "unproven" as nonsensical. And yet, we know that seventeenth-century scientific doctrine postulated a body of so-called evidence in favor of Aristotelian geocentricism, the prevailing theory of the universe at the time, which held that the "heavenly bodies" circumnavigated the earth, which was ostensibly at the center of the universe. It seems reckless and arrogant not to at least remain open to the *possibility* that some apparently preposterous ideologies may be founded in truth.

Either way, while I am always open to others having views that differ from my own, I do not intend to argue my "case" with anyone, because this material transcends the mundane, it transcends modern logic, it transcends the thinking of the masses at this time, and I have written this book having run the gamut of my own alchemical transformation, my own truth. Naturally, my journey continues to evolve; as such, I do not exclude the possibility of further refinements in years to come.

Writing in the nineteenth century in *The Secret Doctrine*,[3] Helena Blavatsky, fierce doyenne of Theosophy, provides a somewhat chilling warning that the secrets of the universe should not be placed in the hands of "unworthy persons":

Thus, notwithstanding all precautions, terrible secrets are often revealed to entirely unworthy persons by the efforts of the "Dark Brothers" and their working on human brains. This is entirely owing to the simple fact that in certain privileged organisms, vibrations of the primitive truth put in motion by the Planetary Beings are set up, in what Western philosophy would term innate ideas, and Occultism "flashes of genius." Some such idea based on eternal truth is awakened, and all that the watchful Powers can do is to prevent its entire revelation.

...

By no means do I consider myself to be a "privileged organism," accidentally revealing the truth to the spiritually great unwashed. On the contrary, I consider it my responsibility to provide a fuller picture in the face of the many half-truths that I see circulating in spiritual circuits, often purveyed by the social media giants. Part of the trouble is that in the twenty-first century, whether or not we like it, information is extremely easy to access and to consume. Times have changed. And so what we now find is that whereas it was relatively easy to cloister certain types of information within the confines of a privileged few—usually the wealthy and elite of society (and that approach had its own problems)—we now have to deal with the repercussions of 111baby on TikTok teaching the unschooled masses (many of whom are still children) how to curse those whom they perceive to have wronged them, or that anyone can avoid hard work simply by manifesting unlimited abundance (manifestation *is* possible, by the way—it just comes with a list of caveats, which I explore in chapter 1).

My conclusion is that, as in all things, the appropriate balance must be struck. If information must be made available, it must be disseminated responsibly.

For those of the older generations who are concerned about the spread of this knowledge and the problems that this may cause (or has already caused), I suggest that it would be helpful to (1) accept that change is inevitable—this change will have both light and dark aspects, (2) understand that humanity is gradually evolving and must have access to a different kind of information from what was available even forty years ago—spirituality is no longer the preserve of the "special" few, (3) adopt a positive, solutions-focused approach based on constructive action in the present by empowering others to develop wisdom rather than by wallowing in negativity and remaining mired in a past that is simply no longer relevant, and (4) exercise detachment from the outcome of these efforts—even with the best possible intentions in mind, it is not appropriate to try to control others in the exercise of their own free will. The information is presented in a transparent and constructive form, and then it is up to the reader to discern their path. This book will find its way to those who need to read it.

My aim is always to simplify rather than to overcomplicate, to reveal rather than to conceal, unless revelation could result in obvious harm. It is in my view pointless at this time to coyly hide the truth among blinds in the hopes that the reader has the appropriate level of wisdom (and the right equipment) to construct an accurate picture. That method has been common in the occult scene for hundreds of years, and perhaps it has had its place, but it is no longer appropriate. This book is, therefore, designed to demystify and forensically examine the scraps of esoteric information that we do have available to us in a cosmos that is dark with enigma.

Neither is my intention to put a label on this book's audience. This book is intended for anyone who feels inclined to read it—spirituality novices and adepts alike, recognizing that the information that each individual reader needs will uncoil itself from the ethers to reveal itself, sometimes in transformative ways, while other information may go, quite appropriately, ignored or unnoticed.

I offer you what I consider to be the main tools that we need to have at our disposal as evolving humans—an esoteric technology appropriate for the current times. I hope that it will help you move forward with purpose and perhaps inspire in you a set of soul-based objectives for the rest of your life. At the very least, I hope that it will prompt you to reflect on some of the great mysteries that inform our very fertile, albeit challenging, existence as humans.

This book is likely to make some people uncomfortable—unlike most other texts of the mind/body/spirit genre, it introduces some challenging—and possibly triggering—material. It was not designed to reassure spiritual seekers of the inherent joyfulness of human existence or to give readers a crutch to lean on to avoid taking responsibility for their unresolved problems. It was never intended to be a warm and fuzzy manual for self-improvement. Quite the contrary; its aim is to act as an unfiltered clarion call to your soul to start doing the inner work if you aren't already doing so. It also introduces concepts that are not widely known in the spiritual mainstream—concepts that are likely to induce kneejerk-type rejection in some cases where readers want to hang on to safe and comfortable paradigms for dear life instead of embracing the possibility that something new and possibly useful is on offer. Either way, the information is now in front of you, and the singular beauty of being human is that you have free will and the power of discernment. You can choose what is useful to you and what is not—you will ultimately be accountable only to yourself.

ONE

DECODING THE SOUL

Athenian: Then all things which have a soul change, and possess in themselves a principle of change, and in changing move according to law and to the order of destiny: natures which have undergone a lesser change move less and on the earth's surface, but those which have suffered more change and have become more criminal sink into the abyss, that is to say, into Hades and other places in the world below, of which the very names terrify men, and which they picture to themselves as in a dream, both while alive and when released from the body. And whenever the soul receives more of good or evil from her own energy and the strong influence of others—when she has communion with divine virtue and becomes divine, she is carried into another and better place, which is perfect in holiness; but when she has communion with evil, then she also changes the place of her life.
—*Laws by Plato*, translated by Benjamin Jowett[1]
...

I am lying in Savasana on my yoga mat after a rigorous self-practice session. Russia has recently declared war on Ukraine, and I have spent the past week struggling to maintain emotional equilibrium in the face of the suffering of so many people. This latest development in a series of global crises has been particularly difficult for me. Unusually, I have been unable to turn my mind away from it. Mentally and physically exhausted, I am grateful to be lying down after the yoga session. Although I am dimly aware that I should be using the opportunity to meditate, I allow sleep to begin to envelop me.

But sleep eludes me. Instead, I see mental images of my first two childhood cats, whom I loved dearly, who went outside one day and never returned. I see them in the vast sugar cane fields surrounding that early childhood home in KwaZulu-Natal, South Africa. Suddenly I am shown that my two cats died of starvation in those fields, presumably lost or injured.

Back in my yoga room in London, some thirty-seven years later, I am surprised. I question why I am being given this information—why, now of all times, when I am in a state of relaxation. It seems gratuitous, cruel, and arbitrary. The answer comes dispassionately and clearly: as the emotions build, I am instructed in real time to consciously transcend the pain. A teacher guiding their student through the vicissitudes of a tricky pose. Firm and steady. I must practice this technique whenever the state of the world upsets me. Whenever I witness animals suffering. Whenever I am provoked. I must remember to control my responses to unpleasant things.

The lesson is obvious. My life needs to go on, efficiently. I know that I have certain things to do in this lifetime, and I cannot be distracted. If my emotions were allowed to run the show, the delicate threads of the web that I am spinning would unravel, taking me backward. Undoing the Work.

When we succumb to our emotions for too long, there is a risk of becoming enveloped by them, mesmerized, like sinking below the surface of a devastatingly blue ocean and never resurfacing. It takes conscious effort to push the mental body back into life and begin to apply logic. That's the discipline.

That doesn't mean that I am not allowed to process my emotions; it means that when an event pushes my emotional state beyond what I know is balanced, I must make a judgment as to when it is an appropriate time to center myself and revert to a more logical paradigm, when I must tame the primitive part of my physical brain before it triggers an adrenal response from which I may not easily be able to return.

When we understand that we are immortal,[2] energetic beings, housed in a physical body, when we remember who we really are, we can see the trials of our humanity in a different light.

You might rightly ask what the point is of a soul attached to the physical body, yet also somehow separate from it, exerting some kind of unconscious control over a person in ways that seem incomprehensible and completely removed from the physical expression of life that human beings are apparently immersed in.

The answer lies in the individual consciousness of every human being and how that consciousness links into a fundamental drive to grow and evolve, a drive that humanity shares as a group.

As you will see later in this chapter, human beings are inextricably linked to one another through our subtle etheric bodies and to the ineffable source of all things (or "Divinity") through our mental faculties; we are all unique individuals who share a common objective: to evolve. We are unique yet interconnected. That condition comes with pros and cons, since the whole is influenced by its separate parts, for better or worse.

If we think about our physical reality and the limitations of that reality and then ponder how significantly our species has already evolved in technology, we can begin to imagine how much further we have to go in that process of evolution—far beyond what meets the physical eye.

The idea of having a soul in a dense physical body is a little bit like wearing clothes; to many of us, the garments and accessories that we wear are important in expressing our unique personality, yet they don't dictate who we essentially are. We go through different phases, from childhood to old age, and our clothing changes according to personal taste, trends, socioeconomic status, and necessity. We only need to shift our mindset to understand that *we are the beings that occupy the clothing; we are not the clothing itself.*

So, if we think of the body as a high-tech suit comprising a partially awakened consciousness, with the soul as its wearer, it is conceivable that the suit could malfunction. The soul understands that there is a risk of malfunction, and accordingly that the suit needs to be cared for according to its particular needs. And so, when the suit does begin to malfunction, the soul may, if the occupier is willing to do the necessary work, take appropriate steps to mitigate the extent of the damage—or stop it in its tracks, applying the necessary fixes and upgrades to optimize the suit for the soul's needs.

The suit was designed eons ago with a flight-or-fight response that is often out of place in the twenty-first century, when it is far less likely that we will be chased around by carnivorous animals. The suit is a miracle, a biological masterpiece capable of producing other suits. Its mysteries thwarted the greatest minds until the Renaissance. And now that we have sharpened our understanding of the suit, it is time for humanity to take the next step—to look beyond the dense physical body and to revisit the study of the soul, together with the other elements of the mental body, as well as the astral body and the etheric body.

The soul enters the "suit" at some point before birth and leaves the body at or shortly before the moment of death. The soul animates what would otherwise be an intelligent machine; it gives the machine (or suit) purpose. Looked at slightly differently, the soul uses the machine to carry out its purpose, yet the soul and the machine are interconnected.

Prior to incarnation, a person is given a specific blueprint in the lifetime, a set of instructions setting out that person's tasks according to the particular state of the soul (and with individual input from the soul). The mission must succeed in that lifetime, or the person will succumb to stagnation, reincarnating into similar circumstances in the following lifetime. The person's choices in one lifetime will influence their lessons and circumstances in future lifetimes under the Law of Karma.

The organism that is the suit isn't necessarily aware of the soul at any point during the lifetime. Whether or not the person is able to recognize the soul in incarnation depends on the level to which the soul has advanced in previous lifetimes. Once a connection with the soul has been established, it becomes important for the person to learn how to control their personality responses to ensure that their consciousness is able to grow as they become more influenced by a higher wisdom rather than by the lower intelligence of the personality. This presents real difficulties for the machine with its baser animal equipment, as it struggles to make sense of an irrational world in which justice isn't always apparent.

Even where the soul is recognized during a lifetime, the challenges that the person faces in the lifetime may be so great that they may struggle to make the right choices.

Life as a human being is far from easy. We must experience both joy and pain—and not always in equal measures—in each lifetime. Our pain incites growth as we are forced to overcome apparent challenges; our ability to transcend those challenges is influenced by the extent to which we have succeeded in overcoming our inherent weaknesses and by applying a balanced approach to our unruly emotions.

Unlike the physical human body, the soul lives on after death and reincarnates for as long as it needs to achieve the desired state of growth that will enable it to escape the endless cycle of birth and rebirth. In effect, human beings are confined to reincarnation on Earth until such time as we have achieved the growth of consciousness that is necessary for our evolution.

Eventually, over many lifetimes of reincarnation and assuming that the necessary work has been done, the soul is able to dominate the personality; at that stage, the person operates in accordance with their unique contribution to the Divine plan rather than from the purely selfish perspective of the individual personality. By operating in accordance with the wider plan, the soul ultimately ascends to higher levels of consciousness and manifests in other ways to carry out different purposes.

It is important at this juncture to bear in mind that reincarnation doesn't necessarily follow a linear timeline. Our perception of time is a very human construct based on our current esoteric faculties—what most of us do not perceive is that time is a relative concept, and that in some ways, there may be different aspects of the soul incarnating in different forms elsewhere in the universe contemporaneously with the part of the soul that is incarnating in this dense physical body "now."

Equally, it is possible to switch "timelines" during an incarnation, depending on the choices that we make as human beings. If that sounds complicated, it's not—it simply means that as the custodians of free will, if we make a decision that changes the course of the current life path, that change may either be in keeping with the options and goals that we were aware of at the time that we chose to incarnate, or it might be contrary to our original goals (in either case, new timelines may be initiated).

For example, at one time as an experienced mystic, I was struggling to cultivate a regular meditation practice. I blamed this on my demanding legal job, my studies, my time-consuming jobs as a yoga teacher and astrologer, my need to ensure that I had time to train my physical body, my Gemini Moon, etc. Until one day my guides made me aware that I was at a crossroads, and that I had precisely three months to get a regular meditation practice going to maintain a clear channel for the information that I needed to have access to, or my timeline would change, and I would head down a less effective path than the path that I had originally set out on. This message was repeated twice, including out of the blue during a passing conversation that I had with a medium friend.

Once we acquire the perspective of soul, we are empowered to step back and look at our lives with far more objectivity. As our vision of ourselves in the cosmos expands, we can detach from our obsession with the singular expression of physicality. When we are enlightened, it is not the creeping onset of old age that gradually wears us down and prizes away our addiction to the ephemeral things of youth; it is the startling realization that we are playing a long game, and that we need to make certain strategic adjustments in our current lifetime to ensure that we achieve the best possible outcome, using the time that we have *now*. At that point, we begin to acquire the ability to leverage our existence on Earth in all its various expressions, without attachment: we begin to optimize our humanity.

With that realization, it becomes possible to begin to exert more control over some of the dynamics that influence our lives. While we are always subject to the Law of Karma, as I explain later in this chapter, some of the levers for constructive change *are* within our reach. I'm referring in particular to recognizing and dealing with any imbalances and identifying and mastering the "shadow" or repressed self—things like unhelpful emotions and behaviors, such as jealousy and anger, letting go of addictions, releasing harmful patterns by consciously deciding to do things differently, and becoming more aware of the many nuances that lie in between what society perceives as "right" and "wrong." The astrological birth chart is one tool to help us unlock some of those mysteries.

If the human "machine" makes the wrong choices, avoiding growth, the soul fails to evolve in that lifetime; worse, in extreme circumstances, the soul can become injured or corrupted by a dysfunctional machine, calling for long periods of exile in between lives. In some cases, the machine may consciously choose to use its advanced esoteric knowledge unwisely, tempted by the promise of short cuts or glamour or because of unchecked ego. Or because the machine has come under influences that are counterintuitive to the growth of humanity. Either way, the machine drifts further away from Divinity, the Source. We must control the machine so that the machine doesn't control us.

Plato, the fifth-century BCE Greek philosopher, described these failures in the following way:[3]

> But as soon as the stream of increase and nutriment enters in less volume, and the revolutions calm down and pursue their own path, becoming more stable as time proceeds, then at length, as the several circles move each according to its natural track, their revolutions are straightened out and they announce the Same and the Other aright, and thereby they render their possessor intelligent. And if so be that this state of his soul be reinforced by right educational training, the man becomes wholly sound and faultless, having escaped the worst of maladies; but if he has been wholly negligent therein, after passing a lame existence in life he returns again unperfected and unreasoning to Hades.

For those of us who have begun to awaken to the fact that we are more than just physical bodies living nihilistic existences, the truth is an inconvenient one because it implies taking responsibility: there is a nagging sense that we must live with purpose, unselfishly and with discernment. We must exercise our own judgment, free of the influences of the masses; we must seek out the truth, however nebulous, and we must stamp out every self-limiting tendency. There is an accompanying loneliness as we begin to realize that we cannot and must not try to convert our friends and loved ones that many simply do not "see." That loneliness must be effectively managed; it is not the responsibility of others to make us happy or to fulfill the mandates that our souls have set for us.

The ancient yogis tended to tell their students to renounce all material things, and there are many modern mystics and spiritual seekers self-flagellating as you read this over their enjoyment of the material world. The thing is that the exhortation to move away from form does not necessarily mean eschewing your annual holiday or selling your house and giving the proceeds to charity. It really depends on how attached the individual soul is to materiality, what their mission is in the lifetime, and whether renunciation of material things is part of the particular journey. Some of us came into the lifetime with a specific mandate to engage with materiality in all its forms. But there's a difference between engaging with the material world in a constructive way in cooperation with the Divine, on the one hand, and becoming wedded to the things of the world to the exclusion of the Divine thread and one's higher wisdom, on the other.

Some people have work to do in the corporate world, and sometimes that work pays rather handsomely. As with most things, it's a matter of judgment as to whether that path is right according to the higher plan. Cultivating the correct judgment in these matters assumes that the individual has done enough work on themselves so as to have cultivated sufficient self-awareness to identify any points of imbalance (whether through their own diagnostics or through the intervention of third parties such as astrologers).

I can offer an example based on my own experiences.

At one point in my legal career, around the time of a typical midlife crisis heralded by a significant Pluto transit to my natal chart, I thought I'd make a go of partially releasing my career in financial services law to develop a more "spiritual" career—surely, I thought, I was deluding myself in thinking that I could continue doing my "spiritual" work as a city lawyer.

The logic seemed obvious—I had done enough time in a "muggle" job to set myself up financially, and now I must have my epiphany and leave the city for a more meaningful career. It would be a sacrifice of sorts—my ego[4] would need to let go of the notion that my status as a lawyer must determine my identity, notwithstanding five years of study and two rounds of professional exams to qualify me to practice in both South Africa and the United Kingdom. Not to mention the many years of personal angst that I had experienced as I had navigated (with varying degrees of success) the rigors of my particular experience of the legal profession—from bureaucrats and officials determined to make my life hell because I had refused to adhere to a pecking order ordained by bullies and autocrats, to vomiting in my boss's Cessna as he flew us back from a client consultation (before or after he had spontaneously handed the steering to me; I can't remember which), and—far worse—insidious cultural toxicity, deceit, capriciousness, and hypocrisy in the career that I had once been so wedded to.

That was one of the problems; I had been far too *wedded* to it and had inadvertently wandered away from my own spiritual objectives. I always seemed to be swimming against the current instead of with it; I was a perennial fish out of water. I couldn't help but notice how alien I felt in that world. I was convinced that it was time to leave.

In any event, my professional crossroads at that time reminded me of those glassy-eyed professionals in Canary Wharf carrying their Iron Mountain boxes around like zombies the Monday after financial services giant Lehman Brothers had failed over a tumultuous weekend in 2008. It was a dystopian wasteland of skyscrapers, pinstripe suits, and broken dreams. The despair had been palpable to me even before I had seen the headlines. The very air had been thick with it.

Months after that cataclysmic event, I began to read stories about ex-Lehman employees in the *Metro* as I traveled home on the Jubilee Line, having tutted, cajoled, and maneuvered my way through the queues backing up dangerously onto escalators in an overcrowded station. The financial crisis was the best thing to have happened to those Lehman victims, the articles said: they had found their true calling; they had a whole new lease on life. Lehman had given them the push to do what they otherwise would never have had the courage to do. Et cetera.

My own personal crisis did not produce the same results. My efforts to step into a gentler (if not genteel) vocation failed dismally as my new plans to work part-time as a consultant lawyer foundered at the time that the coronavirus pandemic struck a (largely) unsuspecting world.

Bereft of what I considered to be meaningful work, I found myself missing my "day job." Something felt distinctly off. I felt so ungrounded in my Lululemon leggings on my way to teach weekday yoga, before even that preoccupation ground to a halt in the wake of the pandemic. Shoreditch is conspicuously lacking in creative inspiration when the muse has been vanquished. The veil is lifted to reveal a tawdrier reality; the putrid smells, rather than the beguiling street art, thrown into sharp relief.

Ironically, I felt that I was in real danger of veering off the path that my soul was directing.

So, after a nine-month "gestation" period in which I brooded, felt about the edges of the darkness to regain my grip, and cultivated a new plan, I reestablished my "muggle" career, taking on a fantastic role at a fintech. This time I had a clear list of intentions and a determination to find the right cultural fit.

Two years later, I received another inner nudge that it was time to leave. The job was in many ways wonderful, but my soul knew that it wasn't right for me, that I needed to move on to the next chapter. By that time, I had learned to really trust that inner voice, and so I made the move with conviction and much excitement, much to the bemusement of those around me.

Of course, becoming aware of the inner nudges of the soul begs the question "What is the soul?"

OUR MULTIDIMENSIONAL BODIES: VEHICLES OF SOUL

In this section, I invite you to take a metaphysical journey into the mysteries of human incarnation to investigate the primordial, mystical, and multilayered constitution of the human being.

When I was a child, I was constantly frustrated by my inability to get to the bottom of my esoteric makeup and how the universe had come into being (I found the "'Big Bang" theory wholly unsatisfactory). I could sense the presence of something mysterious, but all I had as my reference point was Christian ideology as handed down to me by family members (who, by the way, were not particularly religious). I asked lots of undoubtedly irritating questions (such as "How was God born?"), but the answers always seemed to return to the fact that there are certain things that are beyond the comprehension of our human faculties. In reality, an asterisk should have followed that statement:

*The mysteries of the universe are beyond the comprehension of our human faculties.**

Undergraduate philosophy didn't help me address my existential investigation either—I found it extremely dry and difficult to penetrate because, on reflection, I didn't have the perspective that I now have, having actively developed my subtle faculties over the course of many years. Nonetheless, I sailed through my undergraduate law degree with ease—and with an extremely superficial appreciation of the mysteries that second-year Philosophy had ironically concealed. Decades later, I have gradually begun to piece together only *some* of the building blocks of human incarnation and its multifaceted ecosystem.

In this chapter, we're going to review those building blocks in detail. The point of understanding this material is not simply because it may be interesting; from a

---

*Unless we have developed the ability to penetrate the mysteries.**
**Or unless we make the effort, at the appropriate time, to reveal what has been hidden in plain sight.

practical standpoint, just as it's important that we know ourselves inside out on a mundane level so that we can head off any blockers to our goals and carry out the necessary maintenance and upkeep, so it's essential that we have at least a rudimentary understanding of our esoteric makeup so that we can optimize our *spiritual* growth.

Many of us will be familiar with the notion of becoming "enlightened"; yet, few people appear to truly understand what that means. We can practice yoga every day, practice veganism, read the *Bhagavad Gita*, the *Rig Veda*, the *Sefer Yetzirah*, the *Tao Te Ching*, and every other conceivable sacred text, and yet there is no guarantee that we are actually enlightened. First, we need to understand the *process* of enlightenment. To do that, we must understand what is happening at the level of the soul. And to understand what is going on at a soul level, we must understand how the soul interacts with the three bodies that are available for its use.

If we can understand the different parts and our scope to leverage each one of them, we can empower ourselves to make informed decisions toward our higher purpose instead of unconsciously going about our business and hoping for enlightenment along the way by fluke.

The various layers of energy that make up a single human being hang together by force of will, dictated by the soul, the sleeping overlord, awakened in the physical body after countless incarnations.

THE HUMAN BODY AND ITS PLANES OF CONSCIOUSNESS

In summary, human beings have three main bodies, each operating on its own plane (or level):

1. a physical body, comprising a dense physical body together with an etheric body, both of which operate on the physical plane

2. an astral body, operating on the astral plane

3. a mental body, operating on the mental plane

Alice A. Bailey refers to these three planes (and, by extension, to their various subplanes) as the "three worlds of human evolution."[1] At the zenith of evolution, the magnetic interaction between two polarities on the highest plane, the mental body, brings about union, giving effect to an intense light and a consequent disintegration of the etheric body. A similar process takes place on the connected manifesting group (humanity), as well as on a macrocosmic scale (the solar system) as these systems evolve.

It is important to understand that a plane, even the gross physical plane, is not a location, but a state of consciousness.[2] Even though the reality of these states of consciousness seems to be experienced in a broadly uniform manner by other beings, the space into which we project our desires on the basis of our focused awareness of ourselves, or in the case of more-evolved human beings, what we wish to create, is essentially conscious substance. The conscious substance that informs our environments is itself the product of conscious creation by other beings, as well as the *substance* of those beings, as I discuss later in this book. Bear with me.

The planes on which human beings operate, even at their finest, are the densest (or lowest) part of a much greater system of consciousness. This subject is vast and beyond the scope of this book but is worth bearing in mind.

The Physical Body

The physical body exists in duplicate: one part dense physicality and the other part a subtler etheric double, which is in fact the blueprint for its grosser counterpart. It may help to think of the etheric double as the shadow or prototype of the dense physical body.

The Etheric Body

The Oxford dictionary suggests that one of the definitions of "ether" derives from an "archaic" belief that ether is a highly rarified, elastic substance permeating space and matter. Modern science unfortunately isn't yet able to support such a definition— and authors of modern dictionaries tend not to have the esoteric knowledge of mystics (and even if they do, they are doubtless conforming to the current political imperative).

Mystics are aware that this definition of "ether" holds true; the etheric mirror of the physical body is a conduit for subtle energies to be transferred to the physical body from the astral plane (a nonphysical state of consciousness). We know this because we can penetrate other planes of existence by using our subtler faculties. Practitioners of nei gung and chi gung are also aware of this because they consciously work with the etheric body—as do adept yoga practitioners and healers, among others.

The etheric body has two main functions.

First, it is responsible for energizing the physical body by transmitting vital force to it. The etheric body acts as a conduit for the transmission of energy (prana or chi) to the denser physical body from the astral planes and from other beings and acts as a container for that energy. It is therefore obvious that blockages, stagnations, and energetic toxins can and do directly influence our physical health and well-being.

Energies from other human beings can also be transferred to us via the etheric body because our individual etheric bodies are interconnected as part of a greater collective etheric body, such that we are able to transmit subtle energy and influences to and from one another. We are also susceptible to etheric attachments from other beings that we encounter on the various planes. I deal with that subject in more detail in chapter 4.

The etheric body receives, assimilates, and transmits what is essentially life force from the sun through three important energetic centers in the body to vitalize the body:

■ between the shoulder blades

■ above the diaphragm

■ the spleen[3]

Clearly the importance of taking in sufficient sunlight through these centers cannot be overemphasized, while exercising appropriate caution to guard against excessive or harmful exposure to sunlight. In circumstances in which sunlight is in short supply, one temporary solution might be to work (either remotely or in person) with a sound-healing practitioner specializing in planetary frequencies, such as the Acutonics system of sound healing, who can administer the sun's vibrational frequency through sound to the three key energetic centers. Pure sunlight is always best, however.

The other function of the etheric body is to separate the astral body from the gross physical body until such time as the individual's consciousness is sufficiently developed so as to be able to access other planes. The etheric body therefore plays an important role in protecting the astral body.

Alice A. Bailey describes the etheric body in the following terms:[4]

The etheric body is a body composed entirely of lines of force and of points where these lines of force cross each other and thus form (in crossing) centres of energy. Where many such lines of force cross each other, you have a larger centre of energy, and where great streams of energy meet and cross, as they do in the head and up the spine, you have seven major centres. There are seven such, plus twenty-one lesser centres and forty-nine smaller centres known to the esotericists.

...

The "seven major centers" are, of course, the chakra energetic system (or chakras).

Alice describes the fundamentals of the etheric body of the human being and its relationship to the cosmos very clearly in *Esoteric Astrology*:

Esotericism teaches (and modern science is rapidly arriving at the same conclusion) that underlying the physical body and its comprehensive and intricate system of nerves is a vital or etheric body which is the counterpart and the true form of the outer and tangible phenomenal aspect. It is likewise the medium for the transmission of force to all parts of the human frame and the agent of the indwelling life and consciousness. It determines and conditions the physical body, for it is itself the repository and the transmitter of energy from the various subjective aspects of man also from the environment in which man (both inner and outer man) finds himself.[5]

In the average person, the etheric vehicle is the transmitter of psychic energy, galvanising and coordinating the dense physical body and permitting, therefore, astral and mental control of the personality.[6]

(T)he individual etheric body is not an isolated and separated human vehicle, but is, in a peculiar sense, an integral part of etheric body of that entity which we have called the human family; this kingdom in nature, through its etheric body, is an integral part of the planetary etheric body; the planetary etheric body is not separated off from the etheric bodies of the other planets[,] but all of them in their totality, along with the etheric body of the sun[,] constitute the etheric body of the solar system. This is related to the etheric bodies of the six solar systems[,] which, with ours, form a cosmic unity and into these pour energies and forces from certain great constellations. The field of space is etheric in nature and its vital body is composed of the totality of etheric bodies of all constellations, solar systems, and planets which are found therein. Throughout this cosmic golden web there is a constant circulation of energies and forces[,] and this constitutes the scientific basis of the astrological theories. Just as the forces of the planet and of the inner spiritual man (to mention only one factor among many) pour through the etheric body of the individual man upon the physical plane, and condition his outer expression, activities, and qualities, so do the varying forces of the universe pour through each part of the etheric body of that entity we call space and condition and determine the outer expression, the activities and qualities of every form found within the cosmic periphery.[7]

…

To complicate matters somewhat, Alice tells us that the etheric body comprises "the subtle coherent soul" —the sum total of all the souls of all the atoms that make up the physical body. Yet, it is important to remain mindful of the distinction between this etheric double as part of the physical body with its constituent "souls," on the one hand, and the soul that watches (whether consciously or unconsciously) over the entire individual human mechanism (what Alice refers to as the "pervading" soul).

This chapter focuses on the multiple dimensions of the human being, but bear in mind that all our various layers are reflections of the same layers in other living beings, and that human beings are an integral part of the unified etheric fabric of humanity, which is in turn integrated into the etheric fabric of the cosmos through Earth and other planets in the solar system.

More esoterically, the physical form of a human being is composed of a fiery substance provided by certain living beings or devas. I explore this in more detail in chapter 4.

When a human being is developing their personality and is unaware of soul, the etheric body transmits energy of a denser nature to enable emotional and mental control of the personality. When a human being raises their consciousness to the point that they begin to operate from the perspective of soul, the etheric body becomes the transmitter of soul energy.[8]

The Astral Body

The astral body is separate from the physical body. It is often referred to as the emotional or desire body since it is the seat of our desires and emotions and the center of our sentient responses as human beings.

As the individual consciousness evolves, depending on how the personality responds to its awakening, the soul increasingly gains control over the astral body. The emotions are therefore the gateway to developing the consciousness, and it is of primary importance to develop the ability to effectively balance the emotions. This doesn't mean repressing the emotions—that would have the reverse effect, since the emotions would still be present, only under the surface, and just as capable of causing a state of imbalance. It means having the ability to acknowledge a particular emotion and then to let it go rather than harboring it and lingering in an unbalanced emotional state.

The extent to which the emotions are allowed to have free rein over a person determines the degree of advancement of that person along the lines of consciousness. A person who is able to effectively harness their emotions is much closer to union with themselves, and therefore to liberation (or escape from the eternal wheel of birth and rebirth), than a person who is controlled by their emotions and therefore is wedded to form (or physicality).

In dreamtime, the soul has temporary rein over the astral body, until such time as the consciousness of the individual has evolved to the point that they are fully awake in the spiritual sense, and there is no longer any periodic separation between the soul and the individual's feeling center.

The Etheric Cord

The etheric cord bridges the physical body and the etheric body. This cord is part of the network of interlacing channels composing the etheric body; it magnetically links the physical body with its etheric double to the astral body, and ultimately to Divinity, through a kind of polarization (or opposition of forces).

Some of you will be aware of or have experimented with astral travel. If we examine the concept of that phenomenon more closely, the part of us that travels is in effect the subtle part of the physical body (i.e., the etheric double) joined to the astral body (the desire body).

It is well known that the etheric cord must not become prematurely detached from the physical body; if that happens (such as during astral travel), the result is physical death. This does not mean that we should become fearful of engaging in such activity—simply that we should have a healthy respect for it and approach it with the appropriate intention.

The Mental Body

The mental body is the center of our consciousness; it allows us to think. It is, in fact, our higher self[9] and is of particular importance in the mystery of our incarnation as human beings. This is because our advanced mental capacity as thinkers sets us apart from other animals and from other forms of physical life on Earth. There are different layers within the mental body, the highest of which connects us to Divinity or Divine will.

The stuff of mind or *thought* (what Alice refers to as "manas") gives us the ability to operate as rational beings, to harness the ability to act with discernment, thereby distinguishing humanity from the animal kingdom. Yet, Alice explains, manas also underpins the discriminative faculties of life in general, since each decision—even the decision of the smallest cell to generate energy— "is actuated by mind of some kind or another."

Manas is fundamentally electricity; it operates through a system of attraction and repulsion. Our very existence depends on it since we manifest into being through electricity that emanates from our higher mind (the causal body) on the mental plane of the solar system.[10]

The mental plane is responsible for building and containing the physical plane. According to Alice, this is the basis of the concept that we humans identify as time.[11] By "mental" plane, I mean a plane of existence composed of manas, the stuff of mind. That mental substrate is a higher dimension of the physical brain and taps us directly into higher cosmic planes.

Despite its apparently abstract nature, the mental body is material in the same way as the denser physical and astral bodies are.[12]

The mental body manifests itself through the higher mind or causal body, which plays an important role in the ability of human beings to manifest into being, to evolve, and to develop their consciousness.[13] There are three focal points of energy or "permanent atoms" within our causal body or mental substance—the mental unit, the astral permanent atom, and the physical permanent atom. These three permanent atoms (which include the mental unit) correspond to the lowest three levels of the seven planes of the solar system (the physical, emotional, and mental planes), which together represent the cosmic *physical* plane. This pattern repeats itself on higher levels and is worth reflecting on, since even when articulated in a simple way, this concept is highly abstract.

Why Mindfulness and Meditation Really Matter

The very mental process of exploring and understanding our esoteric makeup is important in helping us fulfill our potential as human beings in this lifetime (and beyond) *because the process itself puts us in touch with higher levels of creation.* So, when we merely focus our attention on the mental plane, we can develop the ability through meditation to connect to higher beings.

Manas or the stuff of mind is the link between the lower and the higher elements of incarnation. Manas carries the vibration of the "cosmic mental plane,"[14] the fifth or spiritual plane. This is significant since it implies that human beings have the latent ability to operate on a higher plane merely by leveraging mind, simply by thinking or—as the ancients taught us—by "concentration" (in Sanskrit, "dharana").

This clues us in on the power of meditation: by participating in the vibration of the mental plane merely by focusing the mind, we can consciously open the door to the mysteries (and potentially avoid the problems that come with unleashing partially developed thoughts, as I explain later in this chapter).

The trouble is that the ancient yogis never really explained *why* it is important to be able to control the mind. They simply told us that concentration is a virtuous skill to master, and expected us to simply obey their instructions without question. That method is, of course, anachronistic in the twenty-first century. It's not enough to tell some students that meditation is a good practice to master and that it helps to reduce anxiety and depression. The aspirant yearns to understand the *detail.*

Taking the theory a little further, the fifth-plane vibration is mystically connected to "the Word" that initiated the universe itself. Human beings can leverage that process on a microcosmic level by engaging the spoken word or by vibrating words, including by way of mantra. A word (which is a sound) issued on the mental plane with the appropriate intention becomes contained; it solidifies and becomes a creation. Think about the implications of *that.*

As a yoga teacher, I encounter a common complaint from students: that they are unable to still their minds. Often, they articulate that difficulty in the context of savasana; they are simply unable to relax or lie still. There are always a few students who fidget within a minute or two of lying down on the mat after a rigorous asana (or physical yoga) practice. I am always surprised that rather than almost immediately bringing themselves back to a seated position, they do not opt to simply go to sleep—or at least mirror what they ritually do as a precursor to actual sleep.

Unless there are underlying physiological issues, feeling the need to do the opposite of being still is a sure sign of an unruly mind. And an unruly mind is potentially a dangerous mind. In the absence of physical discomfort, the acts of fidgeting and sitting up also demonstrate an inner resistance to stilling the mind. An undisciplined mind will keep a person imprisoned in the lower nature and its accompanying unbalanced emotions. At a mundane level, a restless mind that simply cannot be still outside the sleep state is extremely difficult to deal with.

If we're honest with ourselves, refusing to take responsibility for taming the mind is a form of laziness. If we are mentally aware of the pitfalls of a mind that cannot be controlled, we owe it to ourselves to put in the effort to address those shortcomings. I am not referring here to mental health conditions; I am referring to the more general need to take responsibility for necessary mental maintenance and upkeep in the longer term if we want to optimize the current lifetime in incarnation. Meditation and mindfulness are critical maintenance tools.

Now, one could argue that those who are resistant to quietening the mind are simply not "spiritually" ready for meditation. But it is incorrectly reductionist to say that they are being "protected" from premature spiritual development by apparently lacking the desire to meditate. Because what most students do not appreciate is that by merely engaging in the practice of yoga (or in any other energy-based activity), they are opening the spiritual floodgates by moving energy around the body. Some students may already have access to psychic skills; those students are at even greater risk of danger should they refuse to learn how to control the mind. I explore those risks in more detail in chapter 8.

Far from merely exerting the physical body and stretching the muscles and connective tissues, the ancient yoga poses were themselves designed to achieve certain esoteric outcomes—the poses mirror sacred shapes, potent with energetic potential.

In a spontaneous vision, I was shown the flow of electrical energy or prana circulating through the body of a person moving through a series of yoga poses. As the person moved into the different shapes, the very specific lines of the poses enabled the effective flow of electricity through the person's body. The source of my vision showed me that this electricity is necessary to optimize the distribution of solar energy critical for human functioning. When, through injury or a sedentary lifestyle, our bodies do not facilitate this flow of electricity, we deprive ourselves of vital energy, and the consequences are stagnation, illness, and physical and psychic weakness. Of course, yoga is only one method of achieving the effective distribution of vital energy—if yoga isn't an option, other methods, such as acupuncture or sound healing, should be explored.

The process of moving energy necessarily triggers an awakening in the practitioner of yoga over time. I have seen that phenomenon in the most esoterically disinterested students, who, a year after consistent practice, begin to report observing "lights" and leaving their physical bodies in savasana. If they do not harness their awakening responsibly by conscious efforts to meditate (ideally under the instruction of a genuine spiritual teacher), they put themselves at risk. Not only do healthful mental habits allow us to live more peaceful lives, but they also permit us safe entry to higher fields of consciousness.

The key to an effective meditation practice is first and foremost to exercise a specific intention to master it; then the student must consciously practice, even if only for a minute or two at a time, noticing any thoughts and emotions that potentially make themselves known, as well as any sensations in the dense physical body. This is mindfulness.

An excellent beginner's exercise (which I learned from my first yoga teacher) is to sit or lie down quietly, consciously relax the body, and use the imagination to visualize a candle burning brightly. The mind is distracted as it watches the flickering flame and intervening thoughts eventually begin to diminish. With practice, the student can start by visualizing the candle and then switch the visualization to complete darkness by mentally snuffing out the candle; this exercise provides a blank canvas on which colors and images may begin to appear over time. At this stage, mindfulness has evolved into meditation.

Many students tie themselves up in mental knots trying to force something to happen in meditation; yet, the solution to the riddle is in the letting go as the mind watches the candle flame or the blank canvas. So, the mind is at once concentrating on holding the space free of mental interjections and critical commentary from the external life, and letting go of expectations of what may appear.

More advanced practitioners of meditation can subsequently move on to vision work, which is a deeper form of meditation in which contact may be made with other beings.

The realm of thought is also where manifestation occurs. We humans have literally been dreamed into being by Divinity via the mental plane. As microcosmic versions of Divinity, we ourselves have the ability to create. An unruly mind will unconsciously create monstrosities; a focused mind will create with deliberate intent. I discuss that process in detail later in this chapter.

The Mind and Divine Will

Just as the astral body becomes increasingly dominated by the soul as we evolve, so the mind becomes more influenced by Divine will as the process of enlightenment unfolds. When I refer to "Divine will" in this sense, I am referring to Divinity in the sense of the absolute, perfect being itself, and the evolutionary plan of the cosmos, of which humanity is a part, which flows from Divinity. As we become attuned to that plan, our actions eventually follow suit and begin to align with that will accordingly, so that we become more focused on selfless service according to that higher plan rather than purely on selfish pursuits (which have quite appropriately served us in other lifetimes). In reality, becoming aligned to the higher evolutionary plan is quite different from the mundane notion of relinquishing all worldly possessions in favor of a selfless existence, although one can see how the two relate.

The notion of Divinity may not sit particularly comfortably with those people who particularly value their independence; however, human beings are fundamentally wired to create by bringing forms together in alignment with a soul that is inextricably connected to the Source. To create, we *must* conform with the will of the Source as dictated by our individual souls. At a certain point in our evolution, we will take the notion of cocreation further when we become capable of unifying Divinity and matter to attain union within ourselves as well as with the Source. If we remain separate, solely following the path of least resistance (or matter) instead of working with Divinity, we as individuals will languish in an evolutionary state that is beneath what we are capable of achieving as a group. I discuss this concept later on in this book.

If you think about it, cocreation in alignment with the calling of the soul as it links to Divinity is intrinsically linked to that part of us that is unique; each individual must act out their own personal story to facilitate personal growth. Asserting the will to achieve that objective may well ruffle some feathers, since others may disagree with our views and objectives. At the other end of the polarity is conforming with the masses out of fear or some other aspect of personality, instead of tuning into the higher mind and the spiritual will—the will that is in alignment with Divinity, the higher purpose.

Having consciously eschewed the dogma of organized religion, with (as I saw it) its inherent toxicity, imbalances, and fixation on manipulation and control, I became aware of Divine will quite free of anyone else's influence. Since my late teens, I have deliberately set out to avoid group settings for spiritual instruction. As a young adult, I became increasingly wary of not being given the latitude to be a freethinker in groups. Yet, as my interest in esotericism grew, I naturally felt a need to develop my knowledge in that area.

Despite my efforts to find like-minded groups of people with whom I could share, I found that, first, I needed to be very discriminating about which schools I attended and who my teachers were, and second, that my attempts to be part of groups failed, with very few exceptions. Having experimented with the idea of joining a school for magical (occult) training, I quickly realized that it was not for me. So, I had to piece my knowledge together from my own experiences over time, with the assistance of books and very limited attendance of classes—mostly those with a practical rather than philosophical focus.

I also discovered in my early years that invariably many of my teachers would disappoint me in some way, not because they didn't have the right knowledge or qualifications, but because, in many cases, of their obvious personality imbalances. So, very quickly, I decided to focus on the information that I could glean from those teachers, rather than on my disappointment that they were not operating from a more elevated standpoint.

I want to pause here to emphasize that this experience was mine and was based on my particular karma, and a clear intention at a soul level that I must go my own way rather than leverage group dynamics as a student. You have your own blueprint and must make your own decisions about whether groups are for you. That said, it is always prudent to be wary of the powerful energies that exist within groups and how they can be exploited, putting the individuals who contribute to that energy at risk.

Returning to my personal mandate, at a certain point in what I will loosely refer to as my spiritual development, in the thick of developing my legal career and all the demands on me in that area, I began to experience a strong feeling that I must try to do something more useful in service to humanity—specifically in the arena of spirituality. So, I began to develop a spiritual tool kit of sorts with the goal of service in mind. I also began to feel an increasing sense of compassion for humans and animals.

I often wondered why I felt that way when people frustrated me so often with their selfish, judgmental, grasping natures and their petty insecurities. The herd mentality so prevalent in the world particularly disgusted me. Slow people in the street annoyed me. Poor customer service annoyed me.

Yet, it is wrong to assume that we cannot be of service because we ourselves are imperfect—with some qualifications.

For one thing, we can (in a responsible and compassionate manner) observe and respond to other people's contrasting personalities and behaviors in a manner that facilitates our own spiritual growth.

Since service work is aligned with Divine will, it transcends the limitations of personality (both ours and others'). That doesn't mean that we get a pass on working through our own "stuff"; however, we *must* take responsibility for our actions, knowing that we will ultimately be held to account.

When we hear the inner call for spiritual service work and we deliberately ignore it—or when we engage in spiritual work but choose to take the easier path by refusing to actively work on self-improvement or by using our positions of influence and our spiritual skills for purely selfish or destructive purposes, we will inevitably set ourselves back in the evolutionary process.

Those who regard themselves as "spiritual" teachers but refuse to constantly strive for self-perfection by surmounting the limitations of personality are the embodiment of toxic spirituality and should be avoided by students.

The process of judgment and karma that operates in response to every individual incarnation should *not* be confused with the paternalistic heaven-and-hell model that organized religion has often used to explain in unfortunately oversimplified terms that there are consequences for spiritual inertia (or, ironically, exploited to control the masses for selfish purposes).

In this game, for which we are optimizing our humanity, there is no church to berate us for our "sins" or to subject us to peer pressure to conform to a particular ideology. There is no physical hell to punish and torment us—at least not insofar as Earth is concerned. Our challenge is to be strong —and *aware*.

Moving in accordance with Divine will means that we must make certain sacrifices as we are put (somewhat unceremoniously) through the fires of spiritual initiation. Enlightenment in its true sense will continue to be a lonely path for individuals until there is a critical mass of humans who are awakened to that cause and humanity collectively shifts into a higher vibration.

The Soul

Equipped with a broad understanding of the three different bodies that make up the *vehicles* at the disposal of the soul, we can now turn our attention to the soul itself.

Soul versus Spirit

The word "soul" is often used interchangeably with "spirit." While it is technically correct that each of us has a spirit, the two concepts are distinct.

First, the term "spirit" is not fully substitutable with "soul": one's "spirit" sits within a broader hierarchy of one's soul. In other words, the spirit is a subset of the soul. Just as the soul resides esoterically in the body, so the spirit resides within the higher dimensions of the soul, linking us directly to Divinity.

Alice A. Bailey explains that at some distant point, each soul will reunite with Divinity (what she refers to as "God"). She says:

> *Man's spirit is one with the life of God and is within him, deep-seated in his soul, as his soul is seated within the body. This spirit will in some distant time put him en rapport with that aspect of God which is transcendent, and thus each of son of God will eventually find his way to that centre—withdrawn and abstracted—where God dwells beyond the confines of the solar system.*[15]

...

Alice is not the first author to have put that idea forward. In *Journey of Souls*,[16] Dr. Michael Newton gives a fascinating account of his studies of patients under deep hypnosis who travel back to previous incarnations and to the "spirit" world in between their human lives. Some of his records of hypnosis sessions with clients include discussions with his clients' guides (sometimes referred to as "spirit guides"), who articulate through the subject under hypnosis a similar idea of souls eventually merging with the Divine.

Second, given the link between the higher "spirit" part of the soul and Divinity, it is not difficult to see how other higher beings are similarly connected to Divinity. It is, therefore, not surprising that we commonly refer to these other beings who mediate Divine wisdom to us (whether or not we are consciously aware of that) as "Spirit."

Yet, this terminology is slightly ambiguous since it incorrectly implies both that we are communicating with the Source (Divinity) itself, and at the same time that we are communicating with one or more higher beings who are also connected to Divinity, whereas, in fact, we are communicating with these higher beings.

Technically speaking, these higher beings *are* connected to Divinity, but it may be less confusing to refer to higher beings as spirit *guides* to make it clearer that we are not *directly* communicating with the Divine—in the same way that when these higher beings communicate with human beings, who are similarly connected to Divinity, they are not communicating directly with *Divinity*. These spirit guides do appear to be of a higher order of beings, however, which is why their job is to guide us.

In a similar vein, when we finally escape the wheel of birth and rebirth as human beings, we are said to "escape to Spirit." And yet, we could argue that because we are already spiritual beings, when we finally transcend our human form, we are merely shedding our physical layers and reembracing our higher "Spirit" nature rather than entering a dimension that is completely new to us.

In summary, the term "spirit" could refer to one or more of the following:

- Divinity

- the higher level of the soul that is connected to Divinity

- a higher being that is also connected to Divinity

SOUL VERSUS PERSONALITY

When Spirit and matter combine, the result is the soul, the self-conscious, thinking entity, or ego. This concept of ego must not be confused with the ego that belongs to the personality. The personality comprises the etheric and emotional (astral) bodies, together with the lower mind. The soul or ego constitutes the thinking entity, which persists through time and space, unlike the personality, which is the temporary vehicle for thinking in a particular lifetime. The personality is in fact the opposite number of the soul.

As souls living a human experience, the goal of humanity is to advance to the point where we are able to transcend our personalities with all their limitations and frailties. That doesn't mean that we no longer experience the highs and lows of human life—it means that we are no longer responding from a flawed perspective— we are responding with the wisdom of the soul, with its direct telephone line to Divinity. One's soul rather than one's personality is in control.

When we reach that point, the personality imbalances subside and the fully awakened soul, remembering who it is, is able to run the show. By which I mean, the stage on which we act out our human dramas, with varying degrees of joy and pain. At that point, drama notwithstanding, the soul attains perfect self-consciousness and begins to be motivated by the higher purpose of service rather than by the purely self-interested demands of the personality.

When there is no further desire to incarnate on Earth to address the shortcomings of the personality or to serve humanity in accordance with the individual karma, there is no further use for the astral or desire body to manifest.

THE BIOLOGY OF SOUL

While the gross physical body is perceptible to the five senses, the soul that inhabits it exists in part on the mental plane and is out of reach of our ordinary sensibilities. As we have seen, the soul is fundamentally composed of the stuff of mind: the soul is in fact mental.

To understand this apparent abstraction (among others), it may be helpful to consider that most of us cannot see the organs, muscles, and connective tissue that sit beneath our skin; nor can we see the individual atoms that vibrate together to make up a foot or a shoe. Yet, those things exist despite the limitations of our sensory apparatus.

Taking the analogy further, we can see the distant, incandescent stars in a clear night sky; we can see the sun, the moon, and, from time to time, some of the other planets in our solar system. But our vision is of course restricted by geographic limitations—by distance, by technological capability, and, if we are talking light-years, by linear time itself.

Now let's introduce the notion of dimension to complicate this slew of variables. And let's factor in the limitations of our understanding of physics.

Mystics understand what modern science continues to grapple with: that other layers of reality exist in parallel with the physical dimension. What this means is that, without the ability to perceive the dimensions beyond our physical perception, it would not be possible to locate the soul by simply dissecting a human body and forensically locating the soul as a collection of minute particles somewhere in the physical being as we currently understand our physicality, no matter how sophisticated we have become at dissecting atoms.

The soul inhabits or—perhaps more accurately—is pegged to the physical body in an entirely different dimension, which is in effect a subplane of the physical plane. So, our forensic equipment would need to be able to penetrate into an ultraterrestrial reality that doesn't currently exist to it.

If you are struggling to grasp the notion of the soul being of a "mental" substance, that's because our current frame of reference as human beings does not have the appropriate capability to give it meaning unless, having developed our psychic faculties, we have been able to explore those other dimensions for ourselves. Our limited vocabulary does not assist us with this abstraction. We must simply accept that the soul is not physical, that it is composed of a finer substance, light energy,[17] and that it exists in a different dimension in "space."

HOW THE SOUL EXPRESSES ITSELF

In the *Timaeus*, Plato, through the voice of Socrates, tells us that the principle of soul is given to us by the Divine and that the physical body is the vehicle for the immortal soul. He explains that the immortal soul is rational and corresponds to the head. He calls this soul the council chamber. He then explains that there is another "inferior" soul located within the body; this additional soul is split into two mortal "souls": first, the part of the inferior soul "which is endowed with courage and passion and loves contention," which he also associates with the faculty of reason, located in the heart, and second, "the part of the soul which desires meats and drinks and the other things of which has need by reason of the bodily nature" (the appetitive soul), which is located in the belly.

In summary, therefore, Plato says that the soul consists of three distinct parts, two of which he says are mortal.

One obvious question seems to be why these mortal or inferior souls—the emotional and appetitive souls—should qualify as aspects of the soul at all.

Alice's description of "the three expressions of the soul" is perhaps a more nuanced (and arguably more developed) version of Plato's description of the three parts of the soul and offers more granular insights into these questions.

Alice suggests that the human soul is the product of the union of Spirit (in its divine sense) and matter;[18] she tells us that every atom, molecule, and cell has a soul, but to a lesser degree than an animal. Similarly, every animal has a soul, but to a lesser degree than a human being.

I will refer to these "lesser" souls as "micro souls," and to the overarching (or pervading) animal and human souls as "macro souls."

Human beings are generally differentiated from lesser beings on the basis of our sense of detached self-awareness. Alice suggests that the soul of every living being is an appropriation of what she calls the world soul (which is also a "macro soul").

As a result of the interaction between the macro or micro soul and the form that it inhabits, a peculiar degree of "quality and sentiency" are expressed, depending on how evolved the body is.

The macro soul is responsible for galvanizing the body along the path of self-development, toward a higher purpose, according to the mission hardwired into the soul blueprint.

In the case of human beings, Alice explains that the soul is the principle of mind—a combination of the lower mind and the "higher spiritual or abstract mind." So there appears to be some overlap between the "mind" as I've described it earlier on in this chapter and the soul.

Alice tells us that the soul expresses itself in three ways:

- through the individual souls of atoms (the micro souls), which cumulatively make up the physical appearance

- through the Personality, comprising the etheric or vital, astral or emotional bodies, and the lower mind

- through the spiritual being (presumably "spirit" or the higher mind, equivalent to Plato's council chamber or "immortal soul")

Once a human being manifests on the mental plane, the three higher elements of the nature of the human being then use the personality or the lower elements to give the higher elements the *experiences* necessary for the development of what Alice describes as "perfect self-consciousness." The three lower elements allow humans to be in contact with the lower three planes.

With this understanding, we can begin to understand the human condition: why our lives seem to be beset by problems, why merely existing often seems to be such hard work, and why we appear to have been "given" a very specific tool kit together with unique circumstances within which to perfect our self-consciousness.

The six elements that compose these experiences are as follows:

The higher elements of the nature of the human being (the causal body)

- the spiritual will

- the intuition

- the higher mind

The lower elements of the nature of the human being (the personality)

- the etheric body

- prana (vital or life force)

- the astral or emotional body

- the mental body (the lower mind)

The element above the highest of these three higher elements is Divinity: what Alice refers to as "the Monad" (or pure Spirit).

THE SUBTLE FIRES

Another important aspect of the multidimensional human body with its various layers is the subtle "fires" that fuel it. These fires are microcosmic reflections of their counterparts in the wider solar system.

When all three of these subtle fires eventually combine, the result is liberation from incarnation in matter and escape to spirit, the end of the cycle of incarnation as a human being.[19]

Active or Emanating Fire
(Fire by Friction[20])

Kundalini or Serpent Power

The purpose of the kundalini fire is to animate and vitalize the physical body. Not only is it responsible for powering individual atoms by providing body heat, but it also actively drives the process of spiritual evolution in the individual in the same way that its equivalent in the macrocosmic system drives evolution in the universe. Kundalini is also the medium through which the personality (or the lower aspect of human beings) is able to express itself on the dense material plane. By bringing the abstract personality aspect into contact with physical matter, kundalini allows the spiritual aspect of the human being to interact with the material plane.

Situated at the base of the spine, the kundalini fires use the three subtle energetic channels of the spinal column and the nervous system to radiate heat out to the body. These three channels are referred to in the Hindu tradition as the Ida, Pingala, and Sushumna. Housed (etherically) in the spinal column, they are the most significant of the many energetic pathways responsible for circulating prana (the vehicle for vital force) in the body. The Pingala pathway is associated with the sympathetic nervous system and the left hemisphere of the brain, while the Ida pathway is associated with the parasympathetic nervous system and the right hemisphere of the brain.

Prana (Chi)

We know that the physical body has a double: the etheric body. In the same way that the dense physical body is vitalized by kundalini, the more subtle etheric body is fueled by its own active system of vitalizing fire or electricity.

The *vehicle* for distributing this active fire is prana (also known as chi). Prana secures emanating light and heat from the sun and transmits them to the physical body via the spleen. This solar energy from the sun is essential for our well-being (but, as we know, can be dangerous in large quantities).

The spleen has a special relationship with the spine, ensuring that the fires of both the physical and etheric bodies are properly blended, and that the body's energetic fuel (prana) is effectively assimilated. Well-functioning physical and etheric fires are important for optimal health (albeit not *solely* determinative of one's overall health condition, as I discuss in chapter 3).

Mental (Solar) Fire

The function of mental fire is to animate the mental body in the human being. We can identify this type of fire in our inherent *will*.

Alice describes this mental fire as "the spark of mind" and "the thinking self-conscious unit or the soul," which is governed by the law of attraction, and is responsible for cyclical soul growth, eventually driving the soul's return to Divinity (the "Monad") through the process of reincarnation.[21]

Mental fire corresponds to solar fire (or cosmic mental fire) in the macrocosm.

Electric Fire (the Divine Flame)

As spiritual seekers, we are often told that we mirror the Divine, but no one ever explains the precise reasoning for that assertion—the best we can do is to accept it conceptually on the basis of pure intuition.

The notion of electrical fire offers us the germ of understanding of the mechanics of that theory to help us ground and assimilate it.

The Divine Flame in the case of the microcosmic human system embodies the highest vibration of the Divine or pure Spirit; this type of fire is the expression of our godlike qualities, since the Divine resides within us.

The purpose of the Divine Flame is to give effect to the evolution of the soul—think of it as the switch that triggers the alchemical process of soul development under the supervision of the mental fire.

REINCARNATION AND KARMA

Reincarnation

(Prior to Socrates's execution)
On entering we found Socrates just released from chains, and Xanthippe, whom you know, sitting by him, and holding his child in her arms. When she saw us she uttered a cry and said, as women will: "O Socrates, this is the last time that either you will converse with your friends, or they with you." Socrates turned to Crito and said: "Crito, let someone take her home." Some of Crito's people accordingly led her away, crying out and beating herself. And when she was gone, Socrates, sitting up on the couch, bent and rubbed his leg, saying, as he was rubbing: How singular is the thing called pleasure, and how curiously related to pain, which might be thought to be the opposite of it; for they are never present to a man at the same instant, and yet he who pursues either is generally compelled to take the other; their bodies are two, but they are joined by a single head. And I cannot help thinking that if Aesop had remembered them, he would have made a fable about God trying to reconcile their strife, and how, when he could not, he fastened their heads together; and this is the reason why when one comes the other follows, as I know by my own experience now, when after the pain in my leg which was caused by the chain pleasure appears to succeed.
    —*"Phaedo," in Plato: Complete Works, translated by Benjamin Jowlett*[1]
                    ...

In the early hours of a cold morning in seventeenth-century London, a man went about the grisly business of disposing of a body. His back was crooked, as was his nature, and it was clear from his demeanor that this task was not new to him.

His face was permanently imprinted with a disagreeable expression, unkindness instilled within him over the decades since his boyhood through perennial hardship—and a measure of innate meanness that issued from a dark heart.

His unpleasant appearance contrasted strangely with many of the women who worked under his direction in the stew, offering sexual entertainment as part of the hospitality provided to customers frequenting the house.

One of these women had become an inconvenience of late, putting up fusses with well-to-do customers who had overstepped her boundaries, rather than simply acquiescing like the others. A high-ranking official had recently been on the receiving end of her insolence. He had threatened to make trouble for the house, leaving the man no choice but to assure the official that he would see to the problem immediately. The woman's insouciance had made his decision an easy one.

Her dead body now lay before him, cocooned in linens and secured by ropes.

It had been much like putting an unruly animal down—unpleasant, but necessary—and he had gone about the job perfunctorily, neither revealing nor experiencing any emotion.

...

Much like the others whom he had dealt with in a similar way over the years, this body would be tossed discreetly out the window into the Thames below, to be carried away by the silent waters.

That snapshot of a past life in which I had been the unwitting protagonist, the prostitute who would not countenance her abuser, was revealed to me somewhat prosaically in the early hours of the morning, my usual viewing time for what I refer to as dreamtime visions.

It had been a particularly busy time for me at work that week, leaving me very little opportunity for self-reflection, never mind more "creative" pursuits.

I had, in the week before I had that particular dream, summarily terminated a significant relationship with two people after arriving at the conclusion that there was simply nothing there; that the relationships had irretrievably broken down many, many years ago, and that in continuing to go through the motions, I was inviting dysfunction, martyrdom, and negativity into my life, which, I concluded, was not in keeping with the blueprint of my soul.

But that didn't make it any easier for me. It was probably the most difficult decision that I have ever made. But I knew that it was the right decision at the time. I have no doubt that my decision caused others pain. But equally I knew that I needed to be strong. Staying aligned with one's true center can be, frankly, alienating.

So perhaps it was no coincidence that I had been reminded that week of another lifetime in which I had had to make a difficult decision—when enough was enough. Maybe I needed to be reminded about what I had to learn in that past life, and the sacrifice involved, so as to increase my resilience in the current lifetime.

The theme of prostitution is an interesting one: To what extent are we prepared to sell ourselves out in the interests of some kind of perceived "good"; to what extent are we selling our souls?

On waking that morning, my husband immediately told me that he'd had a "weird" dream about me—"something about sexual abuse."

How did I know that (1) the dream had been a past-life vision and that (2) it related to me? I just *knew*. I knew in the same way that a "psychic" receives messages from the deceased or about their client's quixotic lover. I too am a medium and very familiar with the past-life arena. This is one significant way in which my spirit guides communicate with me.

In certain circumstances, merely "knowing" something in the absence of empirical evidence implies that one is leveraging skills that modern science would, in its ignorance, balk at. The tricky part is figuring out which of the various messengers are trustworthy among the array of beings that one is likely to encounter when one is energetically open to communication from them. Knowing whom it is safe to open one's proverbial door to is a very important skill. I discuss that issue in detail in chapter 4.

My husband's similar dream had also served to validate the authenticity of my vision—and to reinforce its importance. That type of phenomenon is not uncommon— our spirit guides convey reinforcing messages to us through other people.

Although the vision was completely unexpected (as they usually are), it also made a lot of sense, since I have always sympathized with the work of prostitutes, and I innately understand the value that they add to human society in its current stage of evolution.

So then, what exactly are we referring to by "reincarnation"? Precisely what is happening when someone reincarnates?

First of all, let's be clear about what reincarnation is. Actually, let's not be completely clear, because we don't have all the answers. So perhaps let's lower the bar a little and settle on a few (anecdotally) tried-and-tested basics. As I said before, there is no scientific evidence in support of these matters, so until science catches up, those who haven't had personal experiences to back up these theories will inevitably be left speculating.

Many of you will be aware that reincarnation is firmly embedded in the philosophical doctrine of a number of religions. Yet, fundamentally, reincarnation is a secular construct.

When death occurs, the physical body ceases to be vitalized, and the soul lives on, usually incarnating again in another time and in another body. Sometimes there is a connection between successive incarnations, particularly where there is a soul family connection; sometimes there isn't. Having left the physical body and returned to the spirit world, the soul is allocated a new role, a new experience in the ongoing human drama.

There are various nuances to this process.

For example, having perfected itself through an unfathomable number of incarnations, a soul at the end of its human journey will eventually leave the cycle of incarnation on Earth and merge fully with Divinity before it emerges again in a different form, but always retaining its unique characteristics.

And as I mentioned earlier on in this book, reincarnation may not operate according to our linear perception of time.

As I explain in chapter 8, there are serious consequences for souls who err so badly that they need to be removed from the process of human incarnation for an entire solar epoch. When I say "err," I am not referring to occasional poor judgment or greed or petty crime; I mean the conscious act of choosing to work at cross purposes with Divinity by refusing to participate in the evolutionary process.

By the time a soul has incarnated into a new body, it has temporarily forgotten many if not all its previous experiences. This amnesia is deliberate. In the absence of forgetting, new incarnations would be far too easy, bearing in mind that the goal is for the soul to learn by experience, rather than to "cheat" by skipping ahead a few grades.

Part of the work for souls incarnating as human beings is to refine themselves through the highs and lows of life on Earth. Navigating those two different polarities is what makes the human experience so challenging. Many of the soul's incarnations as a human being will be spent in ignorance of its own divinity; the reason for this is that in the initial stages of refinement, the soul, clothed in a human body, must focus only on developing their personality. Once the personality has been actualized after innumerable lifetimes, the incarnating human is given the opportunity to begin to "remember" their immortal existence as a soul and their connection to the Source. As the human being expresses itself and evolves in subsequent lifetimes, so the challenges and responsibilities increase, and the soul, increasingly resilient, is subjected to increasing trials and initiations before it finally leaves the human cycle completely.

Shakespeare was right: all the world is a stage in the case of the human soul. The drama is in some respects an artifice. As real as it is to the suffering human, it is all a construct to encourage the soul to develop to the point that it is of a sufficiently refined substance so as to escape to Spirit, moving on to the next stage of development. For now, we are—for all intents and purposes—trapped on Earth until we graduate from the cycle of death and rebirth. Or we have consciously chosen to return to Earth as an act of service even though we have long escaped the endless cycle of birth and rebirth.

A further nuance to the process of reincarnation is that in many cases, remembering—with everything that would imply—is likely to be too overwhelming for an average soul, short-circuiting the delicate etheric body attached to the physical body. As I explained earlier in this chapter, the etheric body is the more subtle part (or energetic double) of the physical body, through which an array of energetic forces are transmitted and received.

Some ancient texts suggest that other living creatures, such as animals, also reincarnate. Those beings must work their way up a particular hierarchy until they reach the human stage of their development, when the focus is on developing the mind and self-consciousness. Plants and minerals evolve in a similar manner, as do other beings.

When a human soul has reached a particular point in its evolutionary process, it begins to be permitted access to its past-life memories—either spontaneously or with the assistance of trustworthy psychics or those who specialize in the area of past-life regressions. At that point, the soul is deemed to have reached a sufficient level of proficiency so as to be entrusted with that information, which may then assist it in taking the next step forward in its development. Growth at a soul level, rather than at a personality level, then begins to accelerate.

For example, an advanced soul may begin to be inexplicably drawn to new places or feel a peculiar affinity to certain cultures or even specific people. They may begin to recall details of previous lives, or dream about them. Phobias and sensitivities may have no rational explanation in the current lifetime, but past-life regression could lead to unexpected discoveries that just make sense.

If you have received any "clues" about your own past lives, it may be worth exploring them (with an appropriate degree of caution and under appropriate supervision unless you are adept in that area) when you feel drawn to do so—that may be the missing information that you need to act on in the current lifetime to move forward on your path.

For some people, exploring their past lives could help them process unruly emotions that are unnecessarily blocking their spiritual progress (and no doubt causing health problems, as well as the etheric body beginning to inevitably malfunction under the emotional strain). It could also help with relationships, which are similarly instrumental in the teaching process.

As some of my past lives with my husband were gradually revealed to me over the years, the particular relationship dynamics in operation between us in this lifetime became extremely clear to me. The patterns are uncanny, yet they make perfect sense. Our past lives together have also revealed—through at least one lifetime of oppression in which we were forced to be both resourceful and duplicitous to survive a dictatorship—why we are both so focused on personal autonomy and cynical about politics, and why we work together well in strategic undertakings.

Karma

A significant key to the mystery of reincarnation lies in the Law of Karma, which holds that a person or entity's current circumstances are determined by the sum of all of their past actions—a past that predates their current incarnation.

The soul must work over countless lifetimes to reverse the process of karma by stripping away the denser energetic layers that keep them Earth-bound. The astral or desire body plays an extremely significant role in the process of karma reversal, since it is our desire to actively choose between "pairs of opposites" or different polarities (such as choosing to drop our unhelpful habits or not) that determines how quickly we can reverse our karma.[2] These pairs of opposites are linked to the primordial notion of justice—all actions must be accounted for; all things must come into balance.

The West has learned about karma mostly through the Hindu and Buddhist religions, and to be fair (pun not intended), it seems to have attracted something of a bad reputation. Many modern teachers and thinkers resent the idea that karma implies that they don't have full control over their lives. So, they actively seek to discredit it as hocus-pocus. That's kind of funny, since they *must* be consciously aware that there is so much in the logical world that is undoubtedly out of their control, and *that* seems to stress them out a lot less. Being run down by a bus in a moment of distraction, for example. Or being struck by a rogue bolt of lightning on a golf course. Ironically, the longer they reject the doctrine of karma, the longer they will continue to suffer incarnations in which they will *actually* have less control because they haven't figured out what they need to change at a soul level, their particular "problem."

Karma is far more of a slow-burn phenomenon than the media currently gives it credit for—it may help to think of it in "net" and "gross" terms. Our net karma is what is affecting us *today*, but our gross karma is what we are actively *generating* today (and which will affect us in future lives). Karma is in essence an expression of the law of cause and effect or Divine justice.

We may *appear* to experience instant karma when we engage in misdemeanors in our day-to-day lives, but here's the thing: First, we need to be cautious about what we label as a misdemeanor, since our actions *may be out of our current control*—they *may* be linked to our net karma as accrued in other lifetimes. Part of that karma may be interacting with the karma of those with whom we choose to relate. Good judgment is essential here, however, since we cannot simply relegate our actions to our karma; we must always take responsibility for the part that we play in our actions.

Taking responsibility means knowing ourselves inside and out, and continually working through any toxicity. The more we have purified ourselves of imbalances, the better the position we will be in to exercise that judgment. We can't truly see when we are blinded by the sludge of our shadow selves—something for the "woke" masses to ponder when they criticize others more than they engage in necessary self-examination.

Second, what appears to be instant karma may be linked to actions in previous incarnations (and, therefore, predetermined). So, it is erroneous to assume that where there is a cause, the immediate consequences of that cause are the *effect* of that cause. As I said earlier on, we are in this for the *long* game.

There are a couple of additional factors to throw into the mix.

Karma is ancient in origin, and human beings cannot escape it.

Our karma is partly the karma generated by ancient civilizations. We can trace it back even further though—to events that occurred before the current solar system.[3] It is therefore impossible to divorce ourselves completely from the human situation, its current state of evolution, its (considerable) baggage, and its limited self-help tool kit. We are the product of our ancestors and the dynamics that preceded them.

There are many layers of karma, which vary according to the particular physical form that a soul finds itself in. In the case of the human being, the frequency at which the form vibrates is very slow and dense at the beginning, in its initial incarnations. None of us can avoid those beginning stages; we must all traverse them.

When the soul first incarnates as a human being, it has very little discretion as to the decisions that it makes, since it is in effect trapped in a body that is barely human, a body that is closer to an animal, with its associated animal desires and reflexes. The process of reversing karma begins very slowly, therefore, and gradually speeds up as the soul begins to evolve, attaining its fastest pace between the time that we become aware of the soul and the time that we are finally ready to leave the cycle of human incarnation.

Self-consciousness implies karma.

When a soul has reached the point at which it is able to exert a material degree of influence over the desires of the physical body, it has attained self-consciousness and is, therefore, able to make considered decisions by employing its mental faculties and by applying thought.

The moment a soul becomes consciously aware of the different options available to it, it becomes responsible for the consequences of its decisions. If it then continues to take the easier way out of challenging circumstances (for example, by always acting in a manner that is selfishly motivated) or it actively denies the "work" that it has been given in a particular lifetime toward self-actualization, the result is karmic deceleration and eventually stagnation—the same challenges will continue to present themselves in subsequent lifetimes until the lessons have been properly assimilated.

Where a soul consciously works to interfere with others' karma (for example, by employing "black" magic to attack them energetically, or by deliberately causing harm to others), the consequences for the soul will be far more severe, as I explain in chapter 8.

The point at which a judgment can rightly be made that a person is inappropriately interfering in another's karma is tenuous, and purporting to play judge, jury, and executioner is dangerous since things may not always be as they seem. Interfering in other people's situations—especially when one is purporting to take the "moral" high ground—should be avoided unless there are very good, objectively sound reasons for doing so, always measured against the highest good. As the soul is purified and begins to operate at a higher frequency and from a less selfish, more compassionate, and more elevated place, it is usually able to make better judgments of that nature.

The danger always exists that a person who has some spiritual knowledge, but neither the experience nor the track record to back it up, having not yet sufficiently worked through their "stuff," purports to insert themselves into other people's circumstances or to make judgments or pronouncements on matters in society in a way that is more harmful than good. Again, genuine self-reflection is helpful in these situations, but that assumes that the person is sufficiently self-aware so that they know when to rein themselves in.

Given the lack of self-awareness and self-examination that is so prevalent in humanity, due to our differing layers of karma and our varying degrees of development (even in so-called "spiritual" communities), we can naturally expect a certain amount of wrong thinking to be in operation at all times in society, reinforcing the need for each of us to remain mindful of our own spiritual compass, our own calling, and—critically—the need to engage in independent thought at all times. There are innumerable examples of so-called leaders causing others untold harm. It is important to always question what we are told. Herd mentality is anathema to spiritual progress.

When it comes to judging one's own actions, the guiding principle should always be to ask these questions:

a. Are my actions actually causing anyone harm?

b. Are my actions aligned with the blueprint of my soul as revealed to me through my connection to my higher wisdom?

c. Am I working in the light and for the highest good, or are my actions aligned with the opposite of the light?

When in doubt, meditation, seeking insights and assistance only from those beings who work in the light, may be helpful.

Our karma is a riddle that we must actively work to solve.

Each and every soul has been given a set of tasks to undertake during the course of a lifetime, on the basis of their net karma. That net karma must also be read in the light of the soul's collective karma. For example, if a person's net karma in a particular lifetime is to learn how to stop being a pushover in relationships so that they can develop the ability to be more self-directed, they, like all other human beings, must also deal with the fact that they inhabit a gross human body, with its particular genetic limitations (such as not being able to fly unassisted), and living in a world that is very much the environmental, economic, sociological, and geopolitical product of the humans who have lived there before.

An obvious question is this: How do we figure out what karma we need to address, on the basis of our individual blueprints?

There are various ways of solving the riddle.

The answers could come unexpectedly through moments of illumination, because they are predestined to do so as part of that person's particular blueprint. Or they may unfold more slowly, over the years, through ruthless self-examination and by holding the clear intention to develop spiritual awareness through purification of self, no matter the cost to the ego. It could be a combination of these two processes. The important point to note is that once the awareness is present of the need for soul growth, the process of evolution begins to accelerate and personal accountability is activated.

There are various tools that may be employed to assist the process of solving the riddle. One obvious tool is the astrological birth chart, which reveals an individual's innate skills and talents but also throws the inevitable challenges into sharp relief and reveals the necessary direction of travel from a soul perspective. Other divinatory tools, such as the Tarot, may also be used, with the proper judgment and, where appropriate, with the proper guidance.

I cannot emphasize strongly enough how important it is to apply discernment when employing divinatory tools. If you are going to seek help from higher beings, it is essential that you ensure that they are generally operating from a higher vibration and for the highest good rather than from greed, self-aggrandizement, or some other toxic motivation.

Anyone who accesses information from other planes or through other beings is susceptible to less elevated influences, including from those beings who deliberately set out to misinform and deceive them or exploit them, potentially with the specific intention of causing them harm.

If the mediator of such information has not sufficiently purified themselves, they are likely to be operating from a lower, fear-based frequency and may attract beings who likewise operate from a lower frequency. In that case, the information that they access is likely to be far less reliable (and therefore more dangerous).

If, for whatever reason, you end up in a situation where you are the recipient of information being transmitted by someone whose ability to be a truly clear channel, free of unwholesome influences, is uncertain, it then becomes even more important that you exercise your own judgment as to the relevance of the information that you receive. That relies on you (1) knowing yourself completely and (2) having some ability to discern what resonates with you at a soul (as opposed to personality) level, so that you can reject information that is clearly inappropriate when examined through the lens of your own connection to Divinity.

As will be obvious to you, approaching a situation from a position of soul is the most elevated and powerful position that a person can adopt. Those who have not yet developed that skill are far more susceptible to self-sabotage and interference from lower-vibrating individuals and other beings.

As the individual human actively seeks refinement, for example, by purifying themselves of unhelpful attachments and habits, by operating from a place of unconditional love and compassion, and by ingesting higher-vibrating foods such as fruit and vegetables more often (and, where possible, by avoiding lower-vibrating foods such as meat), their energetic frequency increases, and so they are able to access higher levels of initiation. As they access those higher frequencies, they may also be given access to occult knowledge that they may not have previously been able to cope with or handle responsibly.

Operating at a higher frequency also means that the individual learns how to access the heart center, such that they will begin to experience a higher, more ubiquitous form of love and that they learn how to relate to others (and, critically, themselves) with compassion. Some signs that an individual has begun to access their heart center include feeling genuine love and compassion for other beings and animals outside their own immediate circle, and becoming viscerally affected by beauty of all kinds in a way that transcends the gross physical body. There are two qualifications to be made here.

First, the ability to operate from the heart center in a more transcendental manner does not automatically mean that the individual is beyond reproach as a human being; they will continue to work through their own "stuff"—they are just doing so from a generally more elevated and wiser place (which, of course, means that they have greater responsibility to proactively work through their issues).

Second, when I refer to unconditional love and compassion, I mean the ability to make more elevated judgments, with panoramic awareness, rather than reacting from the perspective of the wounded personality ego. I do *not* mean allowing abusive situations to persist.

For example, it may be necessary to speak your truth in a direct manner in the interests of self-respect, but to do so with the understanding that the other's behavior is coming from a place of fear and insecurity. Although the other's actions may seem to be a personal attack, they are really the product of a far more complex set of dynamics, which the other person may not have developed the ability to recognize or to work through effectively, given the particular stage of their own spiritual development.

The answer is not to try to reform the other person or to force them to see things differently (that is a fool's errand and is inappropriate), but instead to give them the space to follow their own path and to make your own decisions accordingly. Over time, they may begin to change; they may even begin to see you as role model for their own personal transformation. You can share your wisdom with them when they ask for it, but only when *they* are ready, no matter how destructive their behavior may appear to be toward themselves. They must have reached the point at which they are ready for constructive spiritual growth before you get involved.

On the other hand, walking your own path might mean making a difficult decision to leave a person or situation because they or it no longer serves you—or it might mean taking some other equally challenging action. It could also mean staying in the situation but implementing very clear boundaries or accepting the situation's limitations, staying closely attuned to whether the situation resonates with you or whether you are sabotaging your own journey by clinging to the familiar because it is easier and safer to do so.

It is very important to be able to distinguish between your own highest good and the other person's highest good, and to recognize whether your intended actions and reactions are really necessary or are being motivated by your personality (such as a yearning for what you alone perceive to be "justice"). One's "highest good" means that which serves us from the perspective of soul, as influenced by Divinity. It is not our responsibility to interfere in a person's fate by purporting to redress perceived injustices; if we take the Divine Law of Cause and Effect into our own hands by reacting from a place of personality to make ourselves feel better, to assuage our pain, knowing next to nothing about the other person's particular karmic patterning, we are not operating from a place of higher wisdom. That type of behavior will certainly have an impact on us from a karmic perspective. Again, discernment does not imply weakness; it implies wisdom.

When you do choose to offer your wisdom to others, it must never be motivated by a need to control them (for example, to suit your own agenda) or to feed your own ego. It is also important to bear in mind that it can be dangerous to share certain types of wisdom, such as certain types of occult techniques, with people who have not carried out sufficient work on themselves to purify toxic mindsets and behaviors. In those circumstances, the danger could crystallize through short-circuiting the person's etheric body (which is ill equipped to deal with advanced energetic techniques since it does not yet have a simultaneous inflow of Divine wisdom to temper the fires). Or the danger could crystallize in the harm that the person could cause to you or other individuals through the exercise of poor judgment or by inappropriately interfering in karma.

THE PROCESS OF ENSOULMENT

And at the end of the first thousand years the good souls and also the evil souls both come to draw lots and choose their second life, and they may take any which they please.
— *"Phaedrus," in Plato: Complete Works, translated by Benjamin Jowlett[1]*
...

While our souls have a measure of control over the physical lives into which they choose to incarnate, Socrates's reference to the drawing of lots (a random selection process) suggests an element of fate or destiny. So, when he says that souls "may take any which [lives] they please," what he really appears to be referring to is a choice from a narrower selection of possible lives that have been filtered out of a matrix of creative possibilities based on each soul's individual karma.

Since the soul is ultimately focused on liberation from the physical world (of form) and escaping to Spirit, it must work to refine itself over innumerable lifetimes. From that philosophical basis, it is not too much of a leap to understand that the selection process implies a measure of judgment as to the particular circumstances that would be conducive to providing sufficient stretch or challenge for the soul in the next life.

Much like the setting of annual performance objectives that will enable an employee to grow within a corporate environment, an advancing soul will approach the process of life selection with wisdom and self-awareness, knowing that an easy journey is unlikely to be able to provide the friction necessary for constructive *soul* growth.

Souls who are at an earlier stage of their development are likely to experience less complex incarnations—their focus is all about developing the basic personality. Such souls may nevertheless experience difficult circumstances. The less complex incarnations may often attract conditions that bear the hallmarks of objective success in the physical world, such as material wealth. Yet, a soul who has deliberately elected to experience a difficult incarnation may also enjoy objective material world success.

The point is that the physical or material hallmarks of an incarnation are not in and of themselves determinative of whether an individual soul is more or less evolved—each set of circumstances is unique; hardship may or may not be visible to the naked eye. Each individual story has been tailored to a particular soul's unique circumstances, on the basis of their net karma.

This is likely to be an abstraction that most of us can only theoretically understand, but the underlying principle can help us better understand why some human beings are born into apparently perplexing and senseless hardship, some not even making it to full-term gestation.

Some people are understandably outraged by the notion that their own suffering—

often the immediate result of another's cruelty—has come about at least partly by the exercise of their own free will. There is a natural tendency to want to look outside oneself for the source of one's pain, and the idea of being accountable for that pain at some level (even if the source of the pain has nothing to do with our own actions in the lifetime) is abhorrent. Yet, adopting a more panoramic awareness of the broader soul dynamics at play will bring healing.

Becoming more aware of those dynamics does not mean becoming a pushover or encouraging others to continue to be destructive, however. It means cultivating a more effective emotional tool kit to help us respond to the challenges. This is particularly significant in the context of the birth chart, which identifies the particular patterns that an individual will experience over and over again in one or more areas of the life. Those patterns will continue to manifest strongly until there is awareness of the wider soul imperative, at which stage the impact of the patterns will begin to weaken as the soul awakens and begins to assert itself more proactively as part of the process of growth.

Even though social inequality and other apparent injustices are rife in the world, the chances are that you have either already experienced it yourself in multiple lifetimes before the current one or that you are destined to experience it again as you progress on your journey. Most people can identify circumstances in their lives that they consider to be objectively unfair and apparently irrational. The best that a person can do in those circumstances is to treat themself and others with compassion, let go of any guilt that they may be harboring on the basis of their own circumstances, and continue to focus on the development areas that have been identified in their current incarnation, as reflected in the birth chart.

If this broad framework seems to imply a hierarchy of souls, that's because there is indeed a hierarchy. What's important is how we perceive that hierarchy. The fact is that more evolved souls have been more-"junior" souls in other lifetimes—they doubtless bear the sting of the lessons that they have learned in those other lives, of the mistakes that they have made, and of the pain that they have experienced.

The soul of a person living in squalor may be far more evolved than the soul of an individual living a life of luxury and apparent contentment. Or the reverse could be true. It is, therefore, a mistake for us to believe that somehow our souls are all equal. This inherent inequality is a function of the differing phases that apply to the souls incarnating into humanity. It is, however, crucial that we accord each other the respect and compassion that we all deserve as souls, regardless of where we are on the growth spectrum.

How you choose to apply your judgment in this matter is a question entirely for you; I will not tell you to avoid comparing yourself to others, because in some cases that may be warranted. However, any tendency to elevate oneself above others purely on the basis of a sense of accomplishment or personality ego, without humility and without knowing with certainty that one has been put through the fires of purification through multiple lifetimes of initiation, will merely set one back in one's journey. Or it may be a lesson in and of itself.

The sooner an individual can identify problematic patterns, the more efficiently and effectively they can identify and stamp out any delusional or self-sabotaging behavior. Equipped with that wisdom, the individual can recognize destructive headwinds coming their way and then take steps to respond constructively to those headwinds before they gather enough momentum to cause damage. A constructive response might mean having the wisdom to identify early on whether a particular condition really serves the individual, however attractive it may appear on the outside—and if necessary, extricating themselves from that condition—even if parting from it causes them (and others) pain.

In the throes of a personal crisis, it is necessary to draw upon all one's inner reserves, pushing through setbacks with fortitude, reinforced by one's awareness of the framework within which all souls are functioning. It is also necessary to draw upon one's personal support network. I am not referring here to one's friends and family (although they may also be helpful). Instead, I refer to one's spirit guides and the other beings who work with humanity—I deal with these beings in detail in chapter 4. The inner support network develops and becomes more manifest to the incarnating human being as their consciousness evolves and they focus their actions on service and the greater good.

A significant objective of a soul incarnating into humanity is to eventually shift its consciousness away from the individual unit and toward humanity's collective advancement. A wise soul has a profound impact on other souls, including those who are still "asleep" in the current incarnation; part of the work is recognizing where and how one can be of service and then stepping up to the plate in the lifetime—the starting point is to redress any personality imbalances.

I am going to pause here and note that as clichéd and self-deprecating terms such as "service" and the "greater good" may apparently sound, they become increasingly relevant as an individual awakens and gains access to higher knowledge; they must then choose whether to continue to focus solely on themselves—perhaps exploiting their skill set to attempt to control others or fixating on the accumulation of material wealth or other physical things—or whether to heed the calling that they will eventually hear to focus on service; the calling that they alone can discern. A failure to honor others' free will and an insistence on form or materiality to the exclusion of service will cause a soul to lose their way, as I discuss in chapter 8.

Suffice it to say for now that I know that I am not a lone voice in sounding this warning; I have read it in the works of a variety of different spiritual authors. Reading it cold may leave one with the impression that the message is irrationally preachy and that it smacks of fundamentalism, much like the religious texts that seem bent on stripping away any enjoyment from the human condition. I never truly understood the rationale until I had cultivated a body of occult knowledge and was increasingly able to access subtler energies and dimensions. I then found myself standing at the crossroads between working exclusively with form and commanding other beings for my own selfish gain and setting an intention to use my skills constructively in service to humanity in ways that I do not always understand (and indeed do not need to understand). I tussled briefly with the allure of a self-serving relationship with what I will very loosely refer to as "magic," but that was overtaken extremely quickly by an overwhelming awareness of the need to be of service. It was an obvious choice to me.

Being of service (if and when that resonates in the lifetime) doesn't mean that we must turn into saints and relinquish all material things (in fact, the reverse is true in many cases): the key is to purify the mind of all imbalance, develop penetrating self-awareness, eradicate any innate weaknesses, cultivate razor-sharp discernment that is completely unaffected by other people's value judgments, learn how to quickly temper the emotions, and steadfastly refuse to interfere in others' free will.

The cynical reaction to the concept of a service-oriented motivation for the evolving soul is likely to be that humans like to feel valued and that a desire to serve others is inherently selfish for that reason. Perhaps that is true for some people on the basis of the individual karma within a particular field of experience. Perhaps it is easier for some people to run that argument as an avoidance tactic to convince themselves that they don't need to do any real work, that they can simply command the forces of nature to bring them material satisfaction, and that there will be no reckoning when they leave the current incarnation. Reckonings are for bible bashers, after all. That is, of course, not the case, as I discuss in chapter 8.

Like it or not, a leaning toward service is hard-coded into the soul and is triggered when the individual begins to awaken in the lifetime. Service usually goes unrecognized and doesn't equate to any feeling of ego-based satisfaction. It simply aligns with the individual's particular gravitational field.

Of course, being of service doesn't always equate with perfection; as long as we are incarnating as human beings, we all are susceptible to flaws, which is why we must also place self-awareness at the focal point of our existence.

I am sure that I am not alone in confessing that other people irritate me in one way or another on almost a daily basis. As an introvert, I need periods of isolation, and I dislike others encroaching on my personal space. But that doesn't mean that I am not totally on board with playing whatever small part I can to help shove humanity as a collective forward and out of its fear-based, herd mentality. I do feel a strange kind of affection—dare I say, universal *love*—for my fellow humans, a kind of grudging acceptance that we are all family, even if I choose not to *like* (or indeed interact with) everyone. The etheric center of that type of love is anahata chakra, the heart center, and when it kicks in, the individual begins to experience compassion and transcendental love as the gateway to higher wisdom.

The *theory* of ensoulment is relatively straightforward: having exercised some degree of choice as to the lifetime into which it is to incarnate, the soul enters the body. But there are deeper layers of this process to penetrate and assimilate to educate ourselves in this apparently abstruse subject. Understanding those deeper mysteries can help speed up the awakening process; it gives us the structure on which to build the substance of our own creations. It also gives us a greater sense of the macrocosmic potentiality that underpins our individual growth as souls.

One obvious practical question is this: At what point does a soul enter a human body? In *Journey of Souls*, the late Dr. Michael Newton[2] documents his discussions with clients under hypnosis who have regressed so far back that they have traveled to past lives and periods in the "spirit world" in between incarnations.[3] From these highly credible accounts, in which multiple clients' experiences can clearly be cross-checked against one another for consistency, it is apparent that the soul enters the body some months after conception.

In case 29, the client (who is between lives) describes how they merge with the baby's physical body in month 5 and then gently sync their mind with the baby's brain. The client describes this merging process as the filling of a void to explain how the integration of the soul is necessary to complete the baby's development.

Alice A. Bailey offers a technical explanation of what appears to be the first part of this union between soul and fetus as the individual ego (soul) manifests through individualization, before it begins to merge with the fetus.[5]. At the time of individualization, when the fire of matter (fire by friction) meets the fire of Spirit (electric fire), allowing for energy to enter from the higher planes, a sheath composed of mental substance is formed. Alice refers to this sheath as the causal body or ego.

Since Divinity came into manifestation by way of electricity emanating from the causal levels of the cosmic *mental* plane, human beings, as microcosms of Divinity, mirror the process by manifesting into being by way of electricity emanating from our causal bodies on the mental plane of the solar system.

As I explained earlier on in this chapter, there are three focal points of energy or "permanent atoms" within our causal body or mental substance—the mental unit, the astral permanent atom, and the physical permanent atom. These three permanent atoms (which include the mental unit) correspond to the lowest three levels of the solar system (the physical, emotional, and mental planes), together representing the cosmic physical plane.

This point of technicality is important in helping us understand just how connected human beings are to the cosmos—we are directly dialed into the solar system and to the cosmic physical plane—we have an impact on the cosmos and the cosmos affects us. This connection is hugely significant not only by way of a broader explanation of how individual souls interact with the cosmos and the purpose of that interaction, but in helping us truly grasp just how well equipped we are to create, both singly and in groups. I mention the solar system and cosmic physical planes incidentally and have kept this reference deliberately simplistic—a fuller explanation would most likely merit an entirely separate book.

It is important at this juncture to appreciate that the "physical" permanent atom is not physical in the sense that we would ordinarily comprehend dense physicality. Instead, that type of physicality corresponds to the etheric planes or ethers, and, therefore, to the etheric body that I described earlier in this chapter. So, while the physical permanent atom is technically "physical," we would not be capable of seeing it with our physical eyes (or indeed with the mundane technology that is currently available to human beings for viewing atoms).

It is the mental unit (permanent atom) or "mind" referred to in case 29 that appears to sync with the fetus's brain via a "silver thread" or "sutratma," which connects the causal vehicle (or ego) with the physical brain[6] at the beginning of a period of incarnation and then withdraws at the point of death. The sutratma makes its entrance[7] at the beginning of a period of incarnation and withdraws at the time of death through the center at the top of the head—the crown chakra. It is not insignificant that this silver thread also connects the individual to the Divine via the causal vehicle. The permanent atoms appear on the sutratma,[8] which functions as a permanent record of the individual's experiences throughout their lifetimes of incarnation.

What we can draw from this detail is that, together with the antahkarana or rainbow bridge, the crown chakra is hugely significant—we can directly access Divine information through it, and we need to keep it clear to ensure that our connection to Divinity is not obstructed in any way. There are various ways of maintaining this clear channel, including through visualization, color therapy (such as Aura Soma), essential oils, chi gung, tuning forks, and pranayama[9], and by physically stimulating it through the (responsible) practice of headstand in yoga.

As a yoga teacher, I have observed that many (if not most) students fear headstand on the basis of the mistaken assumption that too much pressure is applied to the head (and, therefore, to the neck). Naturally, a student would need to ensure that they have developed the appropriate muscular strength through the upper body (particularly the shoulders) and the core to adequately support this inversion. Once that strength is developed, the pressure to the crown of the head is relatively light, since most of the effort comes from the core, the muscles in the back and around the sides of the body, and the shoulder blades. Assuming that strength has been developed and there are no medical issues, a student who remains reluctant to perform this posture would do well to meditate on whether there is potentially an underlying resistance to accessing Divine wisdom, since such a resistance is clearly counterproductive to soul growth.

THE LAW OF ATTRACTION

Much has been said elsewhere about the Law of Attraction, but what is currently available unfortunately does not present the full picture, perhaps because it was necessary to introduce the information to humanity in bite-sized chunks, allowing us to take the subject in gradually.

Humanity as it is currently incarnating on Earth is operating under the influence of the Law of Attraction, which concerns Spirit and means that human beings are capable of reaching a point of evolution that enables them to work consciously with Spirit (or to cocreate) to create the forms *that are needed by the soul* (rather than what the personality thinks that it would be nice to have, such as winning the lottery—unless winning the lottery is what the soul specifically needs at a point in time). This attractive work is inherently cohesive and is not available to those beings who have not yet reached the same point of evolution as humanity, as I discuss in chapter 6 and elsewhere in this book.

What that means is that, provided human beings are acting within the scope of what has been mapped out for them according to their karma and they are infusing that purpose with Divinity by cocreating according to the information that flows to them from Spirit, they have the ability to create using the Law of Attraction and their godlike ability to bring their creative "children" to life on the mental plane.

As our powerful thoughts and words feed our creations on the mental plane, these "children" gradually attract the circumstances that we have either consciously or unconsciously summoned to ourselves, since every creation is an idea made of astral substance, ensouled within a physical container (or form).[1]

Our thoughts and words are made potent by way of concentrated focus, such as through consistent meditation and mantra and with the aid of positive emotion (such as gratitude), but also through brooding. Our creations are therefore acutely susceptible to being derailed by the wrong types of emotions, which is another reason why it is so important to maintain emotional equilibrium as best you can, even in the face of crisis, to ensure that you do not inadvertently manifest the polar opposite of what you seek to manifest (bearing in mind that perennial theme of duality that human beings are required to work with).

Against that backdrop, a couple of issues should be mentioned:

1. Each of us has tremendous potential to optimize our humanity by consciously creating our own reality.

We can achieve that potential by deliberately setting our intentions according to what we want to achieve, mapped across to our individual soul blueprint.

The key is to be able to recognize the patterns in our blueprints, including any blind spots, to transcend any bitterness that we might feel on the basis of not being able to have whatever we want, and then to consciously create the realities that we *do* have at our disposal, in the interests of accelerating our growth.

2.   Contrary to popular belief, we cannot create whatever we want with the right amount of focused attention and a positive emotional state; this is because we are *co*creating with Spirit, and so we must create by exercising our desires in an *intelligent* manner—in other words, consistent with a higher plan. That higher plan may result in some odd creations, but that is karma at work.

For example, you could incarnate with a particular practical skill set that allows you to take up the occupation of a medical professional, because part of your blueprint is to learn how to selflessly help others in a way that requires a lot of structure and discipline. However, at some point you may decide to consciously manifest a change that enables you to practice on your own in a remote location because you are also learning the value of self-reliance in the interests of soul growth. Within that paradigm, it may not be possible for you to also manifest a stable, happy marriage with three children for the very reason that you are being required to learn how to be self-sufficient and to focus on a more solitary lifestyle. So, no matter how hard you work on manifesting your picket-fence family, you are liable to disappointment and failure in that area.

3.   In many cases, our conscious and unconscious "children" take on a life of their own. In occult circles, these "children" are called "thought forms," and in some cases they can be used in a constructive manner by adepts who have the appropriate skills and maturity to handle them, as was the case with the original "Golem" created in the Jewish Quarter in Prague.

More often than not, these thought forms are a menace to society. For example, concentrated fear fueled by the unruly thoughts of millions of low-vibrating people and the mass media will take on a life of its own, perpetuating lies, causing global destruction, and sticking around for thousands of years, adversely affecting the karma of future generations. It takes a spiritually adept person to recognize when they are potentially under the influence of a thought form, and to take defensive action by exercising their own free will. When in doubt, meditate and seek guidance from higher beings.

There is a similar risk that a person's unconscious thoughts can potentially lead to their undoing—or at least clutter up their etheric body with half-formed monstrosities, much like the stuff of their nightmares.

If our thoughts and minds are lazy and undisciplined, *if we have not figured out what we actually want*, we are liable to create our realities unconsciously—a bit like having a magic wand at our disposal, but never bothering to actually use it with intention, and then bumbling along at the mercy of those undisciplined thoughts. This is another compelling reason to develop a solid meditation practice—we must develop the ability to keep the mind firmly under control.

Alice A. Bailey describes the phenomenon of destructive thought forms as follows:[2]

> *Finally, having constructed a thought form, the next thing the servant of humanity has to learn is how to send it on its mission, whatever that may be, holding it through his own vital energy in its due form, keeping it vibrating to its own measure, and eventually bringing about its destruction when it has fulfilled its mission. The average man is often the victim of his own thought forms. He constructs them, but is neither strong enough to send them out to do their work, nor wise enough to dissipate them when required. This has brought about the thick swirling fog of half-formed, semi-vitalised forms in which eighty five percent of the human race is surrounded.*
>
> ...

One area of potential risk in this area in modern society is the trend as seen on TikTok of parents gifting Christmas elf toys to their children and then creating skits and story lines around them, convincing their children that the elves are real. Both the adults and the children, who become potent with intention and the desire for the elves to be alive, are creating (very effectively, no doubt) thought forms in these elves by charging them with the mental substance of desire. The propensity for such thought forms to become corrupted or to gain lives of their own outside the control of their keepers (on an individual or collective basis), potentially harming human beings, is self-evident. This may sound like an outlandish suggestion, but it is worth taking quite seriously.

The other side of the coin is of course humanity's ability to create and evolve on a mass scale in a constructive manner.

Another recent trend on TikTok saw content creators describing sudden recollections of what they perceived to be actual events or, in some cases, dreams, of having the capacity to float or fly downstairs.

I myself recall having a similar experience at school as a child in my preteens in the nineties (possibly earlier). I remember being in the habit of gliding down a few stairs at a time—perhaps while holding the banister with one hand. Almost like being on a movable platform or hoverboard. I may well have been dreaming, but the experience feels very real.

I suspect that as humanity as a group familiarizes itself with the possibility of that type of flying or gliding—the ability to transcend matter as we currently understand it, using only our human faculties—we are in effect creating a reality for ourselves in which this will become possible, through thought form creation as a group.

I also see this creative capacity through the medium of thought forms playing out in artificial intelligence and robotics. In an unsettling vision of the future, I was shown a world in which robots were substituted for humans in some public-facing roles. The robots were tasked with taking decisions that required judgment—something that even in that future world, humans were better equipped to exercise. Currency had reverted to bartering, and citizenship was negotiable.

There are two aspects of collective manifestation that it is crucial to leverage to optimize our humanity as a group:

1. recognizing the potential pitfalls of our ability to create our future on a mass scale

2. always checking in our right to exercise free will in our created realities—if it interferes with self-autonomy, it must necessarily be a big, fat "no" from us

DEATH

Knowing others is intelligence;
knowing yourself is true wisdom.
Mastering others is strength;
mastering yourself is true power.

If you realise that you have enough,
you are truly rich.
If you stay in the center
and embrace death with your whole heart,
you will endure forever.
—Stanza 33, *Tao Te Ching*—Lao Tzu[1]

...

Dialogue between Socrates and Axiochus:

And so, Axiochus, you pass away, not into death, but into immortality, nor will you have good things taken from you, but a purer enjoyment of them, nor pleasures mixed with the mortal body, but entirely undiluted by pains. For once you are released from this prison cell, you will set forth yonder, to a place free from all struggle, grief, and old age, a tranquil life untroubled by anything bad, resting in undisturbed peace, surveying Nature and practicing philosophy, not for a crowd of spectators, but in the bountiful midst of Truth.

...

Your argument has converted me to the opposite point of view. I no longer have any fear of death—I almost long for it, if I may imitate the orators and use a hyperbole. I have travelled the upper regions for ages past and shall complete the eternal and divine circuit. I was being weak, but I've got a grip on myself and become a new man.
— *"Phaedrus," in Plato: Complete Works, translated by Benjamin Jowlett*[2]

As part of my ongoing medical astrology studies, I participated in a practicum online with a small group of fellow students from around the world. The session was led by a teacher, Dr. X, who is recognized not only for his PhD credentials in the medical profession, but also for his decades of contribution to the field of astrology.

The purpose of the class was to study indicators of disease in the nativity (or birth chart). In particular, we were getting to grips with Abraham Ibn Ezra's method of continuous horoscopy to examine the entire interval between life and death. Ibn Ezra was a twelfth-century Jewish biblical commentator and scholar born in Muslim Spain.

The intervals of time that astrologers work with in continuous horoscopy include the charts that reveal the potential year and month of a person's death. These charts are identifiable through the use of certain astrological techniques that show so-called "exit visa" scenarios, implying that the client *may* have a say in whether or not they choose to exit life at that point in the incarnation. The charts preceding such intervals will reveal the warning signs of imminent illness and declining vital force.

If there are ethically sound reasons for the astrologer to investigate such a chart—such as pinpointing unhelpful habits that are contributing to a chronic condition, in parallel with appropriate professional medical advice, and assuming that karmically it is not the end of the proverbial road for the client, the odds of the client managing to evade premature death are good.

By "ethically" sound, I mean sound according to the individual astrologer's barometer of what is appropriate in the circumstances, free of dogma and the baser judgments of those who operate only according to the demands of the personality.

The astrologer must have purified themselves of anything that could interfere with their connection to the Divine, such as fear, greed, jealousy, anger, and vanity. For that reason, among others, working in the realm of death is not commonplace in astrology and other occult practices.

Assuming that an astrologer has been given access to these tools, abusing their position will lead to the appropriate rebalancing of the scales of karmic justice.

As I said earlier in this book, the purpose of an astrologer learning such techniques and being able to deploy them effectively for their clients' benefit is to help steer their clients toward improvement at times when they are at medical crossroads, and where not addressing underlying issues could prematurely bring on potentially life-threatening conditions.

These techniques are *not* for the purpose of making unsolicited pronouncements on the expected date of death.

At the start of the class, after a few pleasantries had been exchanged, Dr. X, then sixty-seven years old, casually announced that we would be looking at his own likely "death chart." I looked at the other students' little video boxes on my screen. I couldn't see any other faces, but the shock was palpable.

What ensued was among the most surreal two hours of my various experiences working with astrology, as Dr. X pushed each of us to call out possible signatures of his own future death. His very reasonable attitude toward this exceedingly uncomfortable exercise was that at some point he had to die. "How many more solar returns do I need to go through before I decide this is an appropriate exit point?" he asked us rhetorically.

Dr. X has clearly developed an extraordinary ability to face his own mortality head on, transcending fear and misplaced sentimentality.

For most of us, dying is a very uncomfortable reality. Some of us fear it, and for others, it is a phobia.

Yet, at some point, the physical body must grow old and eventually die. Initially, the body will start to fail. As it ages, it begins to lose its youthful elasticity, it becomes drier, colder, and more brittle, and infirmity sets in. It becomes more difficult to take advantage of physical things around us. Or the mind regresses to infancy and the existential debate fades into irrelevance. Sometimes death is unexpected and seems premature. Through age, sickness, or other circumstances, we eventually tire of our mortal existence because we have done all we need to do in the lifetime, and it is time to move on.

We may become so wedded to our material existences and to our mortal bodies that when we do begin to awaken, we find ourselves both inspired by our burgeoning awareness and, at the same time, terrified of the trials and initiations that we must go through as human beings, one of the most significant of which is death. The sooner we can accept that the physical body is simply a vehicle for experiencing drama in the lifetime to cultivate soul growth, and that the body's many pleasures come with significant contraindications that must be managed with temperance and self-awareness throughout the lifetime, the more we can leverage the evolution of our consciousness.

This may seem to be a distasteful subject to draw out, but in bringing it out into the open space of our consciousness, we can face our fears and prepare ourselves for the inevitable journey that we must all sooner or later face.

The fact is that if we hang on to materiality, we are holding ourselves back from our true purpose in the lifetime, potentially setting ourselves up for another round of exactly the same experiences in the next lifetime instead of moving forward. At best, that could be tedious; at worst, it could be excruciating.

As the well-known saying goes, it is wise to wear the world as a loose cloak about our shoulders; to be in it, rather than of it. In other words, clearly, we need some degree of materiality; to starve ourselves of that in an unnatural and unnecessary way could itself be spiritually limiting. But at the same time, it is necessary to get comfortable with the idea of letting go of our physicality.

In a similar vein, we must train our emotions to prepare for the times when we must let go of the ones that we love. It is helpful in that regard to bear in mind that the people with whom we are very close are often members of our soul group and that we will meet them again between lives and in future incarnations.[3]

As the soul advances and, through eons of incarnation, becomes more awakened to its Divine purpose, the individual human, now spiritually adept, acquires greater control over the exit from the physical body. Depending on the individual's karma, there may be a heightened sense of when it is time to leave the physical plane. In other words, there is greater alignment between Divine will and the will of the soul.

When a person consciously or subconsciously decides that they have nothing more to accomplish in the lifetime, and physical death ensues, the etheric web is shattered in its entirety, causing the physical body to be severed from the astral body. This causes the life to withdraw from the physical body into the permanent atoms on the etheric cord.

Because the etheric body has shattered, it loses its polarization and is no longer attracted to the physical body; it can therefore escape. As Alice A. Bailey puts it,[4] the etheric body "becomes nonmagnetic, and the Great Law of Attraction ceases to control it; hence disintegration is the ensuing condition of the form." She is of course referring in part to the fact that since human beings are capable of thinking their own creations into being, so are we ourselves being thought into being by higher entities.

Since it is no longer attracted to its physical body, the polarization of the ego (or thinking, self-conscious entity, the soul) changes, and it is no longer attracted to its physical body. It therefore withdraws from the etheric body (or double).[5]

Depending on the level of advancement of the ego, it may spend time in the astral realm or illusory place of emotions or skip that state of consciousness entirely, moving directly to the mental plane.

THREE

DISEASE

Not knowing is true knowledge.
Presuming to know is a disease.
First realise that you are sick;
then you can move toward health.

The Master is her own physician.
She has healed herself of all knowing.
Thus she is truly whole.
—Stanza 71, *Tao Te Ching*—*Lao Tzu*[1]
...

I studied the obviously female-shaped candleholder in the hearth as I sat on a sofa with other students in the aromatic Southeast London home of my Reiki-Seichem teacher in the early 2000s. The base of the stone candleholder was a replica of a pregnant belly, the aperture of which housed the candle itself. The figurine's naked breasts were also visible as she held her knees. She seemed to epitomize a pervasive energy of the mother goddess, of safety and of being held, lulling all in her presence into enchantment.

It was the final weekend of a program of training to teach the group how to channel energy to heal ourselves and others. As we had progressed through the training, we had discovered that the techniques were shockingly effective. Without exception, every single one of us had viscerally experienced the energy in both receiving and administering treatments, even though physical contact had been minimal. I can't speak for everyone in the group, but on the basis of my own observations, I was satisfied that those experiences were not psychosomatic, their effects often completely unexpected and independently corroborated by both the healer and the recipient of the healing.

Some of the students claimed that they hadn't even mastered the ability to meditate when they had started the course, yet here they were, at the end of the course, perfectly capable of harnessing and directing potent energies.

That living room was a heavenly place to be in to learn about energy healing, a temporary reprieve from the harshness of life.

"Reiki-Seichem healers never get ill," said our teacher, brimming over with confidence and compassion, "because they have learned how to heal themselves."

"I never get colds."

Her confident pronouncement seemed fundamentally wrong, despite my confidence in her mastery of the healing arts.

I studied her curiously. She seemed very healthy, with a pretty, clear face and a well-proportioned frame. In my view it was reckless to test the Fates, particularly in a position of such responsibility. I wondered whether she had genuinely evaded sickness over her many years as an energy healer. In hindsight, I know that one's propensity to suffer disease is far more nuanced.

I was generally very healthy myself, but certainly not beyond catching a cold once or twice a year as I commuted to Canary Wharf on the overcrowded London public transport, a highly effective system for the incubation of germs, with minimal airflow and maximized space. I wondered whether there was any point in administering a consistent healing self-practice to head off my next cold.

There is currently a misconception that disease and ill health, where not attributable to one's genetic makeup, are conditions that we can control purely by making dietary adjustments, exercising, and maintaining emotional equilibrium, and that serious disease is necessarily a product of failing to gain mastery over one or another of these factors.

It is, however, a fallacy to suggest that spiritual purity or an advanced state of consciousness is a guarantor of good health. The position is, in fact, significantly more complicated.

As I explained in chapter 1, we are the product of our net karma, as well as the collective karma of humanity. It therefore stands to reason that we are more or less susceptible to disease and illness depending on our individual blueprint, as well as the particular point in time in which we incarnate as human beings.

For example, a person may fall ill with a serious disease because they are destined to experience that disease so that they can carry out a particular purpose in the lifetime. The disease itself may have come about as a result of the actions of generations who have come before. No amount of attempting to manage away the disease will help the person avoid contracting the disease if it is their fate to become ill with it. There are countless other examples that could be given, ranging in extremity, but the overriding point is that there is a karmic element to disease.

As discussed in chapter 2, death is ultimately unavoidable. Even if death is "natural" and comes about during old age, the organs will eventually begin to dysfunction, and, in many cases, disease will set in as the soul prepares to leave its vessel. That "disease" is completely necessary to facilitate death, and, unless the person's karma allows them to choose whether to avoid death at that particular juncture, death cannot be avoided simply by applying energy healing and implementing (or perpetuating) a healthful lifestyle.

We do have *some* control over our health and well-being, and to that end we ought to inform ourselves of the points of systemic vulnerability—particularly the etheric body (the energetic double of the gross physical body) and the astral or desire body (through which we experience emotion). The key is to become conscious of the propensity toward illness, as well as the factors that are likely to be driving disease, and then working out what (if anything) can be done about it and what it is pointing to from the perspective of soul. With that in mind, we can gather the necessary resources, including the necessary support network.

With a more refined understanding of the inherent risk of disease affecting each of us in different ways, we can sharpen the tools that *are* at our disposal to avoid as far as possible *unnecessary* health problems, including by employing innumerable so-called "alternative" healing modalities and practices, such as energy healing, Chinese acupuncture, sound healing, chi gung, nei gung, and yin yoga, to ensure that our energy systems run smoothly and efficiently.

It is important to bear in mind the various layers of the human body as discussed in chapter 1, and to familiarize yourself with each of those layers and how they are interconnected and interact with the soul so that you can cultivate awareness of obvious areas of vulnerability and take action to mitigate the risk of disease and dysfunction—insofar as mitigation is possible according to your individual blueprint. A medical astrologer may be able to help you identify inherent medical vulnerabilities in the birth chart and to horizon-scan for sensitive points in future, but is not a substitute for professional medical advice.

Let's take a look at the different categories of disease types, as identified by Alice A. Bailey.[2] By the way, when I refer to "disease," I refer to the full range of disorders and dysfunction that might affect the human body, both physical and mental, whether the apparent cause is viral or bacterial, and whether or not the dysfunction affects the outer structure of the body itself.

1. Individual diseases arising from physical, mental, or emotional dysfunction

These diseases are inherited from a person's past lives, and no amount of health and well-being management in the current incarnation will help avoid them. The only constructive action that can be taken in this context is for the person to proactively manage their response to their current condition so that they can assimilate the lessons, speed up their spiritual growth, and avoid repeating the same mistakes.

Emotionally surrendering to the condition and focusing on the underlying growth themes is key. In some cases, the person may be given the opportunity to overcome the disease in seemingly impossible circumstances. The lesson in those cases could, for example, be fostering a sense of determination, resilience, and willingness to embrace constructive change in the face of disaster.

Of course, there is never any guarantee of a future life free of disease, since a soul that levels up in the current incarnation is very likely to find itself presented with even more challenging circumstances in the next incarnation.

Engaging in brutally honest self-inquiry in the face of illness is an essential aspect of the assimilation process—it is important to ask what the illness is showing you. The answers may extend much further than a person's physical and emotional health. Sometimes disease brings about a "healing crisis" as an initiation into a new role that the individual must take on in the current lifetime.

2.   Group diseases inherent in humanity as a whole

These diseases go a long way back and have their origins in ancient collective karma, which may not be exclusively attributable to humanity. This type of illness may be partly rooted in the decisions of our human ancestors, but it is equally possible that they are the consequence of events that predate our solar system.

Whether or not we contract these diseases (and how seriously they impact us) is closely tied in with our individual karma.

Epidemics and pandemics such as the black plague and the coronavirus are likely to be examples of this group of disease. There has been much speculation about the cause of COVID-19; yet, those who have been targeted as responsible for spreading or even creating the disease may simply be the end product of a chain of events that began eons ago. The consequences of our actions in this decade will no doubt be felt by humanity for generations to come. Our individual responses to the coronavirus will drive the pattern of karma in multiple ways as it is woven into this timeline through the etheric bodies of the masses.

3.   Accidental diseases caused by contagious illnesses

Accidental diseases are contracted through happenstance, by being in the wrong place at the wrong time, influenced by an individual's immune system and genetic makeup (which may, of course, be part and parcel of a person's individual karma).

Energy healing and other preventive measures are unlikely to assist a person in the face of exposure to a contagious illness. The coronavirus is also an example of this type of disease.

4.   Diseases caused by "contaminated soil"

This type of disease is far more insidious in nature. It stems from the viruses and bacteria that humanity has unwittingly allowed to proliferate over the eons through the burial of bodies in dark and moist underground conditions. Some of these microorganisms are ancient in their origin, and their effects have been greatly underestimated.

Alice A. Bailey cites ancient Egyptian tombs and more modern graveyards as obvious places for the proliferation of disease, including diseases that are not known to modern humanity.

An obvious antidote to this type of disease in the longer term is for us to cremate the dead rather than burying them.

5.   Diseases affecting those who are on a spiritual path, where there is an uncontrolled inpouring of energy, and the force cannot be handled

Apart from the serious consequences for the evolution of a person's consciousness, where there is an uncontrolled blending of fires causing a premature uprising of kundalini energy without a tempering influx of higher wisdom through the crown chakra (as I discuss in chapter 8), this situation can also make the person more vulnerable to illness.

6.   Astral diseases

Bearing in mind that the astral body is the desire body and the seat of our feelings, the causes of astral diseases are

■   excessive emotion

■   repressed desire

■   out-of-control desire

■   worry

■   anger

When *Esoteric Healing* was first printed back in 1953, long before the dominance of mass media and social media, Alice had identified that "worry and irritation" are the most common causes of disease, and far more prevalent as "intercommunication between people has increased so much, and men live so much in massed groups—large or small—that it is inevitable that they produce an effect upon each other as never before." She wrote:[3]

The increased sensitivity of the human mechanism is also such that men "tune in" on each other's emotional conditions and mental attitudes in a new and more potent manner. To their own engrossing concerns and worries are added those of their fellowmen with whom they may be en rapport. . . .Telepathically, and also with a developed sense of prevision, men are today adding the difficulties that belong to someone else, or to some other group of thinkers and of people, to the difficulties that may be. It is not sure that they will be.

...

Alice comments that worry and irritation are "highly infectious" on the astral plane, lower one's vital force, and cloud one's "true vision." Citing influenza as a "scourge" with "its roots in fear and worry," she tells us that "the astral conditions of fear, worry, and irritation are so widespread today that they might be regarded as epidemic, in a planetary sense." She says that "once the world settles down to freedom from the present 'fearful' condition, we shall see the disease die out."

This provides a not-insignificant clue as to how society is needlessly contributing to individual illness today. Unfortunately, we appear to be a long way away from collectively freeing ourselves from fear. To the contrary, we are being actively encouraged to fear disease, and in many cases the legislature and judicial system are being leveraged to entrench that position.

On the other hand, it is a mistake to assume that by simply controlling excessive emotion we can safeguard ourselves against disease. We need to work through the underlying karmic lessons that we are experiencing in the lifetime to ward off some astral diseases. And it may not always be possible to see the results of our karmic progress in the current lifetime.

For example, I tend to experience eczema flare-ups out of the blue when nothing is apparently out of whack for me from an emotional perspective, when my day-to-day routines and occupations are on an even keel, and when I feel generally content. A few days later, something emotionally challenging crystallizes in a particular area of my life where I have good reason to believe that I am karmically susceptible, and I realize that my eczema was precognitive in origin—I had somehow psychically intuited the impending drama and astrally attracted the disease before the event.

I have experienced this tendency with other medical conditions as well, and in some more serious cases I suspect that the disease must occur to karmically assimilate the negative emotions associated with the challenging event that precognitively triggered the disease.

My childhood tendency toward gastroenteritis disappeared in my midtwenties because I had dealt with that karma, and I suspect that my post-chickenpox tendency toward shingles was similarly assimilated on the death of someone who had been important in my karmic journey in this lifetime. That person had been a key figure in the events that had triggered my first outbreak of shingles as a seven-year-old; when (unbeknown to me) they died decades later, I had the most severe outbreak of shingles that I had ever experienced since childhood, along with a dream in which I was shown that my experiences with that person in this lifetime were always destined to be difficult and that reconciliation in that relationship was impossible. The shingles cleared up quite quickly, and a few days later I found out that they had died around the time that the shingles outbreak was at its worst.

THE SIGNIFICANCE OF THE ETHERIC BODY AS A TRANSMITTER OR ORIGINATOR OF DISEASE

Since the etheric body is an energetic channel, it transmits disease directly to the physical body. In some cases, however, the disease originates in the etheric body itself.

If the etheric body is dysfunctional, the result is disease or weakness. One type of dysfunction results from energetic blockages. It is therefore of the utmost importance to ensure that our etheric bodies—particularly the seven chakras—are relatively free of blockages, allowing prana or vital force to flow freely between the astral body and the etheric body.

As I discuss elsewhere in this book, different chakras or energy centers are active depending on the degree of consciousness of a person. Some human beings are more susceptible to certain types of diseases and dysfunction than others, depending on the particular stage that an individual is at in terms of their consciousness, their karma, and the condition of their environments (including people whom they consciously or subconsciously choose to be around), as well as how proactive they are in maintaining their health and well-being.

When physical disease shows up in the etheric body, it holds the subtle energy of whatever we have assimilated within our energetic field, amplified by our emotional state. That means that if we remain embroiled in toxic situations, with limited control over our emotional state, we are in effect bathing our subtle bodies in substances that are harmful to us. A particular type of adverse association occurs when contact with other beings causes the chakra system to become overstimulated;[4] for example, through possession. I provide examples of this in chapter 4.

A further type of etheric body dysfunction is what Alice refers to as a "lack of coordination and integration."[5] She identifies three different forms of this type of dysfunction:

1. a generally loose connection between the dense physical body and the etheric physical body (the etheric body), resulting in illness

2. a loose connection between specific parts of the dense physical body and the etheric physical body, resulting in a lack of life force flowing to those body parts,

which results in illness or dysfunction

3. a connection that is generally so loose that the soul struggles to maintain its hold on the physical body, resulting in a tendency toward loss of consciousness and, in extreme cases, susceptibility to obsession and possession (I discuss this further in chapter 4)

These conditions may be addressed through conscious efforts to deal with energetic imbalances and to circulate prana effectively through yoga, meditation, and other energy-centric modalities. It is also important in these cases to ground oneself regularly by interacting directly with nature and by walking barefoot outside (whenever it is feasible to do so!). Coffee and chocolate are naturally grounding substances if there has been a sudden shock or an overwhelming encounter with nonphysical energies and beings.

Since these conditions may not be readily identifiable without the help of those who are attuned to them, cultivating a deep inner awareness as well as self-empowerment through meditation is key. This solution is unfortunately not a quick-fix one; it requires, first of all, the expression of a clear intention to develop awareness in this area and, second, commitment and an ongoing dedicated practice of meditation. As the meditation practice grows, so the person will naturally begin to develop the ability to observe certain phenomena about themselves, often with the assistance of other helpful beings whom I discuss in the next chapter.

The subject of disease is a vast and complex one but is something that we should be keenly aware of, along with the full range of possible treatments and healing practices—first, in the interests of effective prevention (where possible) and necessary personal maintenance and upkeep, since illness is by no means restricted to the dense physical body, and second, as part of our overall awareness of the soul condition.

FOUR

OTHER BEINGS AND ENTITIES

Empty your mind of all thoughts.
Let your heart be at peace.
Watch the turmoil of beings
but contemplate their return.

Each separate being in the universe
Returns to the common source.
Returning to the source is serenity.
—Stanza 16, *Tao Te Ching—Lao Tzu,*[1]
...

T here is something quite wholesome and safe about the notion of a human soul striving for perfection, grappling nobly with the internal influences that might hold it back from escaping the endless wheel of birth and rebirth. Yet, comparatively little seems to have been said in this context about the many other beings that feature in the human paradigm, from the beings that form the building blocks of creation itself to the hostile entities that pervade our societies, willing our destruction—and everything in between. All those entities are an integral part of the hierarchy of the universe that humanity is but a tiny part of.

As human consciousness evolves, it is becoming increasingly important to cultivate awareness of these other beings. Even though they are rarely acknowledged, their influence is real and experienced by humanity both consciously and unconsciously.

The process of soul growth involves moving beyond the confines of the personality and positioning our life goals within the framework of the soul so that our operating system becomes more progressive. And progress means acknowledging that we operate within a far broader system than we could ever have imagined, and that we owe it to ourselves to become more aware of how the actions of other beings in the wider ecosystem affect us, for better or for worse.

Many people balk at the notion of the existence of invisible beings who interact with us, potentially in invasive or disturbing ways. Sometimes they are literally the stuff of our nightmares and invoke a unique fear in us—the kind of fear born of phenomena that we cannot explain away to human vice or mental illness, and for which science has no explanation (and would therefore prefer to dismiss). More often than not, people tend to relegate these phenomena to psychology, ostensibly to give themselves a means of controlling them. Even in occult literature, the subject has been scantily addressed, and where it *has* been addressed, the information has tended to come in piecemeal form.

In the following sections, I address what I consider to be the most significant of paranormal beings, drawing from my own experiences in some cases to provide insights into matters that might otherwise remain an abstraction to many readers.

DEVAS

One of the things that I've noticed while musing over the multitude of religious, spiritual, and philosophical systems, practices, and texts, from antiquity to modernity, is just how many similarities there are between the various ideologies—quite literally floating about in the ethers as they become thought forms, acquiring their own defining emotional charge.

Even where there are material differences (such as the practice of believing in and worshiping a single ineffable deity versus worshiping a pantheon of gods), the commonalities are unmistakable. While each system is susceptible to corruption, the similarities are there if one looks beneath the surface.

I've always considered these similarities to be potentially significant in pointing me toward the truth (or at least validating what I have already discovered myself). I started to notice the overlapping areas as a young adult as I developed my own ideological framework.

Identifying the useful patterns by looking beyond the propaganda, the groupthink, and the banal, and by adopting a softer focus (like those autostereogram "Magic Eye" books in the nineties) helped me process what had begun to unfold within me and what was irrevocably revealing itself. It was too much of a coincidence that apparently dichotomous texts were so uncannily connected. It was as though the darkened rooms within my brain were slowly becoming illuminated.

This process also helped me recognize that organized religion is a socially engineered garment in which human beings have swaddled (sometimes suffocating) universal wisdom—usually to the detriment of the followers of that religion. Despite the obvious fear culture and the thick layers of hyperbole, opacity, and calculated omissions, in some respects religion is a veil for universal wisdom. Religion has had its place in our history. It has served various useful purposes, in some cases by maintaining an authentic link to higher forms of consciousness through certain highly evolved beings or masters, and offering through that link a degree of spiritual protection and aid. Religion also has a more esoteric purpose, which is to prepare "average" human beings for future enlightenment, as I discuss below.

One of the flaws in religion, however, is the expectation that human beings should worship deities, effectively relinquishing to them all vestiges of self-autonomy, rather than recognizing the divinity in themselves and actively working to evolve by reconciling the pairs of opposites in themselves and in the world in which they live, thereby achieving balance. When I refer to "deities" in this sense, I am not referring to Divinity (or the Source); I am referring to a particular category of supernatural, conditional beings. The trouble is that some religious texts don't make a clear distinction.

The reality is that a deity who demands to be worshiped or to be given things in exchange for favors is not a balanced entity—it is suffering from the same imbalance of personality as a social media influencer who is drunk on the heady hit of adoration by their fans.

Where there are apparent exhortations in religious texts to "worship" the Divine, the ineffable Source or "God" (who is often simultaneously portrayed as exhibiting lowly human emotions), it is important to understand precisely *what* you are being asked to worship—and to think about what "worshiping" actually means.

If one is able to detach from dogma, from the recriminations that circulate about the ongoing disharmony between the various systems, and—given humanity's current state of disarray—the pointless calls for unity and world peace, one can begin to usefully assemble a dispassionate and accurate picture of the truth. At least those aspects of the truth that it is permissible for humanity to ingest at this time.

What I'm suggesting is that we pick through the ideological sludge to find the nuggets of spiritual gold and then forensically narrow down all the various options to arrive at those ideas that are consistent, credible, and resonate with our spiritual experiences (unsullied by the limitations of the personality).

I don't particularly like using the word "spiritual," since it smacks of New Age credulity, but it's the closest (in its pure form) to objective "truth" since the other similar words—"religious," "philosophical," etc.—tend to be rooted in a conditional reality and don't embrace every layer of the human condition within the greater cosmos.

Why I bring this issue up here is that this chapter is about "devas"—and the term "deva" is particularly wide ranging, describing a class of entities of fundamental importance to human beings. Wide ranging because devas pop up in a wide variety of historical and modern texts.

The word "deva" has its origins both in Indian and Zoroastrian religion. In Hinduism, during the Vedic period, devas were divine beings (or deities) who were regarded as benevolent—unless they had cause to disapprove of the behaviors of human beings, meaning that they were conditional beings. Zoroastrianism took the opposite view of devas, regarding them as evil. There was a similar dichotomy over another class of deities—asuras—which were generally regarded as evil by Hinduism (apart from in the oldest parts of the Rig Veda) and benevolent by Zoroastrianism.

Devas are important because they permeate every part of our existence on this planet, because they are intricately involved in our makeup and evolution, and because if ignorance is allowed to prevail, some of them will without question set humanity back in its pursuit of advancement, on both a collective and individual level. This has already happened to some degree, but my expectation is that this state of affairs will begin to change as humanity empowers itself through awareness, acquires a resolve in favor of self-determination at an individual level, and becomes less inclined toward a fear-based operating system.

At this point, some of your proverbial eyes will no doubt begin to glaze over as you question the credibility of such a pronouncement. Some of you will wonder whether I am referring to "extraterrestrials" (there is indeed some crossover, which I explore later in this chapter), and others may begin to lean toward an assumption that I am a conspiracy theorist (I am not easily swayed in that direction).

Such assumptions might allow some readers to default to their comfortable, long-held beliefs that humans are pretty much alone on this planet (save for the animals that we have largely succeeded in subjugating), and that any deities that we may choose to entertain within our worldviews are at a comfortable distance from us, to be visited when we are in despair, on Sundays, at Christmas, and such, allowing humanity to go on neatly compartmentalizing our ludicrously dichotomous existences.

Most people who have acquired a reasonable understanding of occult matters are aware at some level that paranormal beings do, in fact, exist. Many people—whether or not they are spiritually inclined—have had firsthand encounters with them in some shape or form, whether through visitations in dreams or meditation, bizarre "coincidences," visceral sightings, psychedelic drugs, near-death experiences, or mediumship (clairvoyance, claircognizance, clairaudience, and so on).

The trouble is that holding a general view that there are other beings out there "somewhere," without any real understanding of their purpose or agenda, who or what they are, and how they can be distinguished from other paranormal beings, is a very tricky position to be in. This risk is amplified in the case of people who actively engage in occult ritual, such as invoking angels, elementals, or demons.

It's one thing to vaguely perceive that other beings exist while being completely disinterested in engaging with them; it's quite another to hold a similarly vague perception and then to actively seek to interact with them without a full understanding of what they're all about.

Occultists who are active in the chaos magic scene in particular are susceptible to such risk if they do not take care to understand the subjects of their magical operations. Summoning a being in ignorance is tantamount to opening the door to one's home blindfolded, in the naive hope that the person who is standing on the threshold of what is effectively one's center of power is offering something trustworthy—

and then standing back to allow whatever or whoever that being is to enter the house and #hopingforthebest.

The same reasoning applies to spiritualist séances or gatherings whose purpose is to interact with paranormal beings (such as Ouija board games), where the group intention has not been assiduously set before the proceedings have begun, along with a full understanding of the type of being with whom the group wishes to interact and consciously attune to.

Some people like to reduce paranormal encounters to psychological aids or to mental dysfunction—after all, it's often far more palatable to assume that they are creations of our own, to give us a degree of comfort that they are under our control. As we all know, unverified assumptions can lead to disaster.

In some cases, these beings *can* be our own creations (I explore this subject in more detail later in this chapter). Sometimes a person who is suffering from mental illness may indeed imagine that they are interacting with another being. These perfectly legitimate scenarios make the subject of devas all the more treacherous and difficult to navigate since they also serve to obfuscate the truth, which is that these beings actually do exist independently of the human psyche. So, what we in effect have in these situations is a convenient blind for paranormal beings who are inherently dangerous to human beings and whom we should never trust. I deal with these beings below.

If we remove thought forms, and recently deceased human beings (popularly referred to as "ghosts") from the list of possible entities who might legitimately be classified as "paranormal," we are left with a variety of beings or devas who are either helpful or harmful to humanity. I am including in my categorization of "deva" all the angels, spirit guides, elementals, and gods (deities),[1] as well as the entities referred to as beings of smokeless fire (djinn or jinn) in the Middle East, Africa, and Asia (or demons in the West), some of which humanity identifies as extraterrestrials. There are doubtless other categories of deva in between, as well as innumerable subcategories of the types that I refer to here.

It is important that we are familiar with the deva ecosystem, since its operation is integral to our own existence and the path of evolutionary growth. Whether or not we are comfortable with the notion of invisible beings permeating our existence, they do, and some of them are antithetical to humanity in the same way that some human beings are destructive toward one another. It's important to consider the whole picture and to understand how each group of beings operates within the bigger paradigm rather than artificially compartmentalizing and focusing only on some beings (such as angels) to the exclusion of others.

We can consciously develop our ability to harness the assistance of the devas where it is appropriate to do so, making wiser choices where it is hazardous to seek them out. We should also become far more conscious of the devas who mean us harm—that is a reality that we need to stop whitewashing and denying so that we can empower ourselves to deal with them effectively when we are in danger.

Most of us are broadly familiar, at the very least from a storytelling perspective, with the concept of elementals—salamanders, undines, sylphs or fairies, gnomes, and the like. There are large quantities of texts on this subject, although folklore through the ages—in many cases backed up by anecdotal evidence—suggests that not all elementals are pleasantly disposed toward human beings.

As the higher chakra centers awaken, it becomes increasingly possible to contact and communicate with devas (such as the violet devas) on the etheric planes. These planes are higher than the dense physical plane on which humanity generally operates. In many cases, the devas operate on the planes of humanity—gas (or mental), water (emotional/astral), or earth (physical)—although they are skilled in the art of glamour or creating illusion and may therefore not always be immediately visible.

A number of authors have attained recognition or even fame for bringing information to light on the devas whose purpose is to help humanity—angels.

After publishing a number of books on this subject for many years, one well-known author and spiritual teacher unexpectedly renounced her work with the angels, to the horror of her followers (many of whom had regarded her as a role model for enlightenment and the epitome of light) and no doubt her publishers, reverting to orthodox religion and claiming that it had come to her attention that her work had really been the product of diabolical influences who had deceived her.

I was saddened to hear of this turn of events. It appeared that the author was, unfortunately, unable to effectively cope with the dichotomy between good and so-called evil; if she had been better equipped to strike a balance between the two polarities, she might have been able to implement suitable mechanisms to filter out the beings, who had clearly been harmful to her (assuming that she was also doing the appropriate amount of work of her own at a soul level). On the other hand, I guessed that part of the lesson inherent in her current incarnation was to grapple with this very theme, perhaps in a very extreme way.

I had always found it frustrating that as helpful and accurate in some respects as the author's work on the angels had been, it had systematically failed to sound the appropriate warnings to those among her considerable audience who had enthusiastically commenced their own communications with angels at the risk of encountering impostor devas—malevolent beings posing as angels.

In a similar vein, every single one of the workshops that I attended on esoteric subjects during the early years of my occult studies, from Tarot to mediumship to psychometry and geomancy, had strangely omitted to articulate the unseen dangers of the occult. The formula was always the same: participants were taught to put themselves into a light trance and to openly interact with any old being that happened to come along.

It was never really sufficient protection to ground ourselves by starting the exercise with our feet on the floor to prepare for meditation (a precursor to the trance state). Grounding is not necessarily protection. Without attaching names to schools, there was an unfortunate political undertone of fear when it came to discussing the darker side of the occult. Everything was sanitized and euphemized— my distinct impression was that they didn't want to scare students away. Or perhaps those teachers weren't properly equipped to teach students about those types of risks.

So, instead, they led students unwittingly toward the edge of a pit of potential destruction. Whether a student takes a wrong turn will depend on a variety of factors: how much wisdom they have developed, their net karma, whether they are already in an unhealthful relationship with a destructive being, whether they are susceptible to obsession or possession—for example, through mental illness, shock, or trauma (leading to a loose connection between the dense physical and etheric body)—or simply how reckless they happen to be. I decided that if I was going to teach, I would do so differently.

In the following sections, I deal with some of the most significant categories of devas (or angels as they are sometimes referred to). They are genderless beings and vary in color, function, and intention, and I highly recommend a deeper study of them.

Alice A. Bailey provides far more detailed discussion of this topic in *A Treatise of Cosmic Fire*[2] and other works, although—apart from acknowledging that destructive beings exist and providing more generalized references to cosmic "evil" —neither she nor Helena Blavatsky appears to have dealt in any depth with the beings that I refer to as "the Shadow People" —the devas who deliberately set out to harm human beings.

GUARDIAN ANGELS (SPIRIT GUIDES)

Some angels are responsible for helping humanity by acting as guardians to us. Every human being is assigned at least one guardian angel. Sometimes referred to as spirit guides, these are the mysterious beings that often appear to humans, typically garbed in white or appearing as beings of light, at times of crisis, such as in near-death experiences. This phenomenon has been documented widely and is increasingly appearing in mainstream media, such as Netflix.

In *Journey of Souls*,[3] Dr. Newton recounts with uncanny consistency example after example of interactions between his clients and their assigned spirit guides. It seems likely that the specific type of guardian or spirit guide differs according to whether the human is in the process of an incarnation or whether they are between lives in the "spirit world."

Alice A. Bailey refers[4] to guardian beings as "white devas of the air and water who preside over the atmosphere." She says that they "work with certain aspects of electrical phenomena" and control the seas, rivers, and streams:

> *From among them, at a certain stage in their evolution, are gathered the guardian angels of the race when in physical plane incarnation. Each unit of the human family has his guardian deva.*
>
> ...

I have become increasingly wary of the nebulous and frankly lazy manner in which occult texts and teachers have dealt with the concept of "guardian angel" versus "higher self" versus "higher intelligence." It is sloppy at best and misleading at worst to fudge those terms. A "guardian angel" does exactly what the name suggests, and it is possible to learn how to communicate with these beings as one develops one's psychic faculties and learns to access the etheric and astral planes.

As I explain in chapter 1, one's higher self is one's higher mind.

The term "higher intelligence" may also have been intended to refer to guardian beings, since the word "intelligence" was historically used interchangeably with "angel," "deva," and the like. However, "higher intelligence" could also be used to refer to the intelligence that one has cultivated at a soul level—in other words, wisdom accrued through experience, similar to one's higher self. To confuse things even more (or perhaps clarify them), that intelligence is materially influenced by solar angels (which I refer to below), who work on the mental plane and are specifically responsible for assisting in a human being's spiritual evolution.

VIOLET DEVAS

Many modern occult sources refer to a particular violet-hued angelic being as archangel Michael and assign to "him" the specific task of protection and the dispelling of fear. Back in 1925, Alice had written:[5]

> *At the beginning of this period of recognition, men will principally contact the violet devas, for those of the higher ranks amongst them are definitely making the attempt to contact the human.*
>
> ...

Anyone who has worked with these violet devas will immediately recognize the connection of their functions to bolstering the astral body's defenses and grounding and inspiring confidence and courage. However, the violet devas primarily concern themselves with the "evolutionary development" of our etheric bodies.[6] Some of them are involved in building etheric doubles, while others form the very substance of the etheric doubles.[7] These devas evolve by working through the mode of feelings or emotions (via the astral body) and are tasked with schooling humanity "in the perfecting of the physical body in its two departments"; namely, both the dense physical body and the subtle physical body (the astral double).

An important example is those deva beings who form part of the sevenfold etheric chakra energy system—they are integral to the process of evolution, and they put human beings directly in contact with the soul of the earth itself through the planets.[8]

I have had quite a few yoga students tell me about their experiences of encounters with violet- or purple-colored beings or "lights" after meditation or savasana. Some don't yet recognize these lights as beings. It is not at all surprising to me that this is a common outcome of a regular yoga practice, since the physical asana part of the practice moves prana or subtle energy around the body in a way that makes it easier for human beings to contact beings of a finer substance, specifically activating the chakra energy system.

The key is—as always—to ensure that whenever one is working energetically (or energetic contact is a possible outcome, such as in the practice of yoga), contact is consciously made with helpful, not harmful, beings. It is important to frame an intention to interact only with beings who are operating for the highest good and to learn the fundamentals of energetic protection, such as clearing one's space before working, visualizing oneself cocooned in golden or purple light, and invoking the assistance of those beings who operate only for the highest good of all.

Knowing that the aim of the violet devas is to help us perfect control over our physical bodies—*and knowing that our physical bodies also include our astral doubles*—is helpful since it gives us an enhanced sense of purpose in our lifetimes. Importantly, it also helps us frame our intentions with far more clarity, since we now know that we are eminently well equipped to create in accordance with the law of attraction. When we put all these various components together, what we end up with is a formula for fast-tracking our evolution.

GREEN DEVAS

The function of the green devas is to protect the vegetable kingdom and those places on Earth in which energy vortices or magnetism occurs—places such as Stonehenge and other sacred places, including many locations on which churches have been built.

It is likely that much of the trouble that ensues when humans experience encounters with hostile fairy beings in nature, such as in cases of trespassing on sacred land, arises where these beings are operating in a defensive capacity to protect these areas, bearing in mind that these devas are conditional beings and potentially very dangerous. It is, therefore, advisable, however ludicrous the notion, to exercise caution as to how one interacts with nature, paying due consideration to where one intends to build or destroy pockets of nature.

Green devas are contactable by way of "magnetisation,"[9] meaning that where a person's etheric web has burned away and they have gained full control over their astral body, they are capable of emitting a magnetic current[10] suitable for putting them into contact with the green devas.

Talk to the beings who inhabit nature before entering their domain, and if you are in any doubt, consult an expert in such matters.

There is clearly an important connection between the integrity of our plant life on Earth and the effective nourishment of our bodies. While many human beings still eat meat, there is a curious hint in *A Treatise on Cosmic Fire* that plant life may become the dominant form of human sustenance up until the end of the current human chapter. Bailey says:[11]

> *For the green devas the path of service is seen in magnetisation, of which the human race knows nothing as yet. Through this power they act as the protectors of the vegetable plant life, and of the sacred spots of the earth; in their work lies the safety of man's body, for from the vegetable kingdom for the remainder of this round comes the nourishment of that body.*
>
> ...

Healing devas are affiliated with the green deva group and are of two main types: First, the elemental of Earth itself, who is in charge of the more powerful lunar devas. This elemental being may be invoked in extremely limited circumstances in connection with healing on a mass scale, such as in the case of epidemics and pandemics. Second, healing devas who will work only with the most advanced, pure, and selfless human beings for the purposes of healing. In those cases, contact must be initiated by the deva or masters rather than by the human beings involved in the healing process. These devas are capable of giving life in circumstances where it is permissible for death to be avoided, but human beings who work with the second category of healing devas will know not to attempt to heal a person where death is indicated.[12]

By contrast, in the case of Reiki-Seichem, practitioners work on the etheric body in cooperation with the violet devas, who are referred to as beings of "the violet flame."

BUILDER DEVAS

Among the more important devas are those devas or elementals who form the building blocks of form itself on every level of the cosmos, including the form of human beings.

Builder devas are essentially fiery in nature, operating within the ethers and transmitting prana or vital force. They are responsible both for building form as well as comprising the substance of the form itself. It is perhaps ironic, therefore, that they are dangerous to humanity, since vital force is inherently fiery and can be harnessed for destructive purposes.

Builder devas operate on a group basis rather than as self-conscious units, and some of them may be controlled by more powerful builder devas or angelic beings higher up in their hierarchy, as well as by human adepts.[13] Ceremonial magic or rituals involving the evocation of these devas should therefore be approached with extreme caution—those who meddle with them in ignorance put themselves, and potentially others, at serious risk of quite literally burning out.

Since the physical form of human beings comprises deva essence, it is important to bear in mind that human beings are in part deva. Likewise, any successful act of creation on the part of a human being involves working with deva beings as the substance of life.

THE ENOCHIAN ANGELS

A perhaps less well-known group of devas were discovered in the sixteenth century by John Dee, mathematician, occultist, and astrological advisor to Queen Elizabeth I, together with his colleague and friend, Edward Kelley. There is a fascinating story to be told about how the mystery unfolded and the strange dynamics that operated between Dee and Kelley and their wives, but what is material for the purposes of this book is that they discovered a system of contacting a specific hierarchy of deva beings whose help can be enlisted for a variety of purposes, both good and destructive.

The formulae involved in contacting these beings are extremely specific and convoluted and involve the use of very particular tools, which the magician should ideally have constructed themself. Despite these apparent barriers, Enochian magic has gained much popularity in recent years, in part thanks to the work of certain occultists who have translated the text to modern parlance and have clarified the methodology.[14] Having said that, reckless dabbling in this practice puts one at risk of evolutionary setback, as I discuss in chapter 8. The focus should be on evolutionary or constructive purposes, with soul growth firmly in mind, rather than the commandeering of these beings for destructive purposes. Appropriate judgment must be exercised in any workings with these beings to avoid putting oneself—and humanity—at risk through hubris, ignorance, or malicious intent.

Alice A. Bailey appears to have directly singled out this class of deva, as is implicit in the following warning:[15]

On a peculiar group of devas who are the agents, or "mediates" between magicians (either white or black) and the elemental forces. This group is occultly known as "The Mediatory Seventh" and is divided into two divisions:

...

a. *Those working with evolutionary forces*
b. *Those working with involutionary forces*

One group is the agent of constructive purpose, and the other of destructive. More need not be submitted anent this group as they are not easily contacted, fortunately for man, and can as yet only be reached by a particular group ritual accurately performed—a thing as yet practically unknown.

...

Despite the inherent warning against working with these devas, we must also recognize their constructive use, the detail of which is outside the scope of this book. For that reason, it has been necessary for the information to come to light and made available for evolved and fastidious human beings.

SOLAR (AND LUNAR) ANGELS

The solar angels are another important category of fiery devas; as beings of the sun itself, they carry out an important role in the development of human beings' individuated or realized consciousness on the mental plane. Having themselves passed through humanity in incarnation in previous solar system epochs, they have attained a higher degree of wisdom and are therefore integral to the spiritual (as opposed to physical) evolution of human beings, to whom they pass on their wisdom.

These angels meet with human beings after death, prior to reincarnation, and it is worth noting that they have an interesting and somewhat notorious history in the chronicles of humanity.[16] Their work naturally conflicts with another group of devas, lunar in nature, who govern the base lunar (or material) nature, the personality.[17]

From a karmic point of view, solar angels were destined to incarnate in the current age to further develop their own consciousness. Eons ago, however, some of them refuted the callings of karma and chose not to incarnate until a later time, with the result that the particular group of human beings into which they eventually incarnated were already corrupt—precisely because the solar angels had procrastinated. The incarnating angels, themselves corrupted in the process, then perpetuated the problem, effectively doing the opposite of helping the affected human beings develop their consciousness, which led to the creation of certain monstrosities, with which other human beings then appear to have interbred. It is not clear what drove these devas to collectively evade their karmic responsibilities (or indeed how that was possible), but it appears to have been a conscious choice.

Some readers will recognize this account as that of the biblical "fallen angels" or Sons of Enoch, also referred to as the "Sons of Wisdom" or "Watchers" (which is closer to their true purpose).[18] In that regard, the more skeptical among you may wish to investigate the various disparate accounts of the ostensibly fabled Atlanteans, including Edgar Cayce's own highly credible revelations of Atlantis, in which Frankenstein-like abominations of humanity frequently appear.

Should they accrue the appropriate wisdom, the cohort of human beings who are incarnating in the current solar system round will eventually incarnate as more-evolved beings in a future solar system following the death of the current one. From there, there is potential for us to carry out these functions overseeing planetary systems that are higher than our current solar system.

THE COUNCIL OF ELDERS

Some years ago, I was surprised to find myself transported in vision to a temple of what I noted in my journal at the time as "intelligences" that appeared to be located on the star Sirius. These beings were twelve in number and introduced themselves to me as "the Council of Elders." They conversed with me very directly on a number of topics, and I have since encountered them from time to time as and when they see fit to engage with me. On occasion, I have specifically sought them out. They are highly evolved devas and work alongside humanity in humanity's best interests.

Alice doesn't say much about these devas (who seem to feature widely in occult literature as beings who operate in service to humanity), although she notes that they have previously incarnated as human beings and that they are "of equal rank with certain members of the Hierarchy," referring to other higher beings in the hierarchical scheme that currently operates in relation to our solar system:[19]

There is another group of devas about which much may not as yet be communicated. They have come in from another planetary scheme, and are specialists in their particular line. They have attained, or passed through, the human kingdom, and are of equal rank with certain members of the Hierarchy, having chosen to stay and work in connection with the physical plane evolution. They are not many in number, being only twelve. Four work in the violet group, five in the green group, and two in the white, with a presiding officer of rank equal to a Chohan. The number of the deva evolution is six, as that of man is now five, and as ten stands for perfected man, so twelve stands for perfection in the deva kingdom.

...

GODS, ARCHANGELS, AND MASTERS

Gods and Archangels

The gods (or deities) and archangels are of very different orders from the devas that I describe above, and warrant separate treatment.

Gods are highly evolved, yet still evolving, conditional beings who issue from the union of the Source and matter and are involved in giving effect to the creative purposes of the cosmos with evolution in mind, as well as to the destruction of those creations. Their conditionality separates them from Divinity, which means that they are subject to imperfection. This may seem abstract, but in fact it is simple: conditional beings are susceptible to behaviors that are unbalanced and are therefore susceptible to error. This imperfection is present because the opposing forces of cosmic good and evil must play out to cause the friction necessary for cosmic evolution.

Seen against this backdrop, the pointlessness of worshiping deities becomes apparent.

Gods preside over solar systems; their function is to give effect to certain principles established by even-higher beings in the cosmos. In the case of our solar system, the purpose of the life cycle of its administering deity is broadly to give effect to the principle of "love-wisdom" through various subsidiary principles. I explain the concept of love-wisdom in chapter 7. The solar god or deity manifests through certain bodies in the solar system, including the sun itself. This is significant when considered in the context of astrology.

The solar system deity oversees seven archangelic beings, each of which embodies and carries out a subset of the principles of the solar system deity.[1]

Archangels—in a similar way to some forms of more powerful devas—are dispassionate and impersonal beings, akin to powerful machines programmed to carry out specific functions. They are vastly different from the violet and white devas, who are tasked with the day-to-day support of human beings.

Deities must not be confused with certain orders of deva who are worshiped as gods by human beings. Those devas are also conditional beings of a much lower order who can be programmed by the skewed will of other human beings.

This brings us to an ancient wisdom that is largely dismissed as dogma (and therefore anathema) by those who are not religious: the worship of form or materiality is antithetical to spiritual evolution. The reason for this is that form is inherently flawed and is the medium from which all human beings are ultimately working to escape.

I am not suggesting that human beings should not enjoy the material aspects of their lives; rather, the warning is to exercise caution against becoming wedded to the substance of form itself by pegging one's spiritual advancement to conditional (and therefore flawed) beings. Or by becoming obsessed with form or physicality to the exclusion of Spirit.

Unfortunately, organized religion has distorted this message so badly that it has now morphed into a corrupt form of moral policing, as we are seeing in the Middle and Far East, as well as in the West.

Masters

Certain highly evolved beings or masters operate in service to humanity and the evolutionary objectives of the wider solar system. Like some of the more evolved devas, they are proficient in the human levels of consciousness, having previously incarnated as human beings, yet have chosen to work with humanity, sometimes incarnating again as human beings, notwithstanding that they have already escaped the wheel of human incarnation and are, in that respect, free spirits. Their role is to use science, religion, and philosophy to prepare average human beings for a deeper understanding of spiritual growth.[2]

These masters are not themselves devas, but they are assisted by a group of devas. They work on spirit rather than on form.

THE SHADOW PEOPLE

In the Arab and Islamic worlds, jinn haunt abandoned houses and crumbling ruins, inhabit caves and sewers and sink-holes, wander through deserts, guard hidden or buried treasures, take the form of snakes and other beasts, possess humans, and perform wonders at the bidding of magicians. But what may seem to be jinn activity is not always so. Even those who believe firmly in jinn concede that swindlers, grifters and scammers often use this belief to manipulate the guileless and defraud the innocent.

According to Islamic tradition, God created angels from light, humans from clay[,] and jinn from smokeless fire. Jinn—a word derived from an Arabic root meaning to "conceal" or "cover with darkness"—are said to have the ability to hide themselves from humans, often by disguising themselves as animals such as snakes, dogs and cats. Many jinn listed to the teachings of the Prophet, found them persuasive[,] and became Muslims. Various local traditions, including those in Palestine and Arabia, also recognise the existence of Christian and Jewish jinn.

—Robert Lebling, Legends of the Fire Spirits Jinn:
Genies from Arabia to Zanzibar[1]

...

Although the jinn often visit mankind of their own free will, there are also many ways by which sorcerers can summon them. These methods, if used closely, may expose them to temptation and peril. For most people in the muslim [sic] world the jinn represent dangerous and demonic creatures, but sometimes they can render helpful service.

It is believed that jinn manifest in human beings through fits of possession. When the body falls to the ground in an epileptic or paralytic fit, it is said that the jinni inside it manifests its presence. Thus, an act of exorcism is needed to evict, or at least appease, the jinni, depending on whether the host benefits or suffers from the spirit possession. This process is accomplished through various rites.

—Rain Al-Alim, *Jinn Sorcery*[2]

...

In the dark hours of early morning in North London, I found myself suddenly transported from my forest-green winter sheets to a dull but crowded airport somewhere in the United States. I had no idea why I was there or where I was supposed to be going. A man approached me on an escalator. He was unremarkable—brunette, middle aged, relatively tall. But canny. His demeanor seemed to fit the demographic of a middle-class professional. Perhaps an accountant or a lawyer. Or a CEO. He looked me straight in the eyes and in matter-of-fact tones asked me how to "deal with" the 'Shadow People.'" He was calm in the way that some professional people are, even when shit is raining down on them. But I knew he had a problem and that he needed a solution. I knew what he was talking about.

Blurry eyed in my London bed, I made a note to try to help him—well, at least those people whom he represented. They needed a crib sheet of sorts, I supposed. The basics on addressing obsession and possession. Fundamentally, they needed to understand *who and what* they were dealing with.

I am by no means the first author to write about the category of deva known in the Middle East as the beings of smokeless fire. There are many excellent resources available on the subject, some of which I refer to in this book, referring variously to these beings as demons, jinn, djinn, devils, evil spirits, and the like. I am offering a slightly different perspective, informed by my own experiences, on what I have come to refer to interchangeably as the jinn or "the Shadow People." That perspective is framed within the wider context of the human soul and its cosmic ecosystem.

When we see the bigger picture, the constituent parts or fragments that we may be only vaguely aware of suddenly acquire meaning. And when we are aware, we are empowered to make more conscious decisions.

The ability to make conscious decisions in these matters is particularly important in the context of the notion of cosmic evil that I refer to in chapter 6. When human beings are ignorant or choose to deny that something is off, they are more susceptible to blindly stepping into problems that might otherwise have been avoided—or at least mitigated. They are also particularly vulnerable to mass manipulation, which is antithetical to the evolution of humanity.

The other side of the coin is that with awareness comes responsibility, since the Shadow People become keenly interested in those who take an interest in them. And so it is necessary to maintain effective spiritual hygiene and an ongoing protective regimen, especially concerning boundaries, to manage the residual risk.

What are the Shadow People?

The Shadow People are mysterious and often-frightening paranormal beings that humanity has been encountering since time immemorial, yet science has been unable to pin down. Their geography is unlimited (although some parts of the world seem to attract them more than others), and they manifest to human beings in a variety of forms. Sometimes they are neutral and merely curious; often they are malevolent and go out of their way to terrorize and destroy human beings. Whether or not they are of a neutral disposition, the jinn have a proclivity for obsessing and possessing human beings. By "obsessing," I mean the act of systematically breaking down the human being's willpower so as to facilitate possession.

If we think back to our own multidimensional makeup as human beings and how the soul enters the physical body after the first few months of gestation, it is not too much of a stretch to see how it is feasible for other beings to enter the human body in a similar manner.

The two different scenarios are vastly different, however, and it's important to understand the difference.

When the soul enters the body in the womb, it does so to equip itself with a vehicle specifically made available to it for incarnation on Earth, and it is born into a particular set of circumstances that will give it scope for growth in that lifetime. By contrast, a jinn who possesses a human being is invading a body that already houses a soul. Unless the human gives permission for such possession, the jinn is interfering with the human's free will. While some jinn appear to possess human beings to experience a richer form of physicality than that which is otherwise available to them, many of them deliberately set out to possess human beings to destroy them.

In *Legends of the Fire Spirits*, Robert Lebling reproduces a fascinating article[3] that appeared on an Arabic internet site in 2002. The article "purported to be an interview with a female jinn who had possessed a human being." The interviewer, a human being, directed questions to the jinn via the human being that the jinn was possessing, drawing out various insights into the jinn paradigm:

Q   **What is your real name?**
A   *Our names are secret and cannot be given. We borrow names similar to your names and keep them throughout our lifetime.*

Q   Where is your location in this world?

A   *Our location is also secret.*

Q   Do you have continents and countries as we do?

A   *No, but we have many kingdoms, kings, princes and peoples.*

Q   Can we know the names of some of those kingdoms?

A   *We describe our kingdoms in terms of colours to bring the concept closer to your understanding, so we say the red jinn, the blue jinn and the yellow jinn, but in reality these colours are expressions of differences amongst us.*

Q   Then you too are veiled from each other as per the type or colour?

A   *Yes, we are veiled from seeing some among us, and we cannot see other types of jinn from other kingdoms, but there are exceptions, as is the situation now.*

Q   Husna Khanum, what is your position in your world?

A   *I am the daughter of the red jinn king, who still reigns over our kingdom.*

Q   How old are you?

A   *Twenty-seven years old.*

Q   Are you married?

A   *No, not married, for your grandmother [i.e., the person talking to the writer] doesn't leave me with much free time. She summons me often to come cure people and solve problems arising from jinn.*

Q   I know you are a Muslim. Do you have other religions?

A   *Yes, we have converted to Islam along with humans and have entered into this holy religion. We have other religions and we have infidels. We are much like you in this respect.*

Q   How are you able to enter our world?

A   *We see and feel you because your density is higher than ours. This can be exemplified by a staircase whose steps go up from the subtle to the dense. This is as regards the physical formation; the basic structure of humans contains all the steps of this staircase, but your sciences have still not attained even a minimal knowledge of the real structure of the human being—till now we're unable to interact with you in a good way except through you, i.e., by entering your bodies.*

Q Can you explain to me how do you enter our bodies?
A *We enter the human body during one of the moments of its life, and at a certain state of it.*

Q What do you mean by a certain state?
A *I mean when the soul splits from the body for a period of time, and then we open a loophole through which we can enter.*

Q When does the soul split from the body?
A *Many are the states in which the soul splits from the body—other than death of course—i.e., temporary splitting, such as during dreams that occur in sleep. The hero of this kind of dream is the soul or the astral body that goes out and flies away.*

Q That means you enter when the human dreams?
A *No, of course not. We can't reach someone through these exitings [of the soul]. If this were the case, it would be easy to enter all human bodies.*

Q Then which state are you talking about?
A *There are many states—quite a lot of them—such as a coma resulting from shock, a fall or a crash, or those that occur due to extreme panic or terror. All such states, in addition to the psychological state of the target person, are suitable for entering a person.*

Q Are there targeted persons?
A *Yes. Due to our structure, we can see you without you being able to see us. By your normal actions you might cause us harm, either intentionally or not. In this case, the person who caused us harm becomes a target for us and we watch him closely, and when a certain entrance state occurs we take the opportunity and enter him.*

Q What languages do you speak?
A *We do not have a specific language. We communicate telepathically [with each other], but through you we speak your languages, which we learn through our interaction with you.*

Q Can you tell us about your social life?
A *Yes. It's very similar to your life [as humans], especially after you [humans] die.*

Q   In reality, we don't know anything about the shape of our life after death, except through the philosophies we study.

A   *When you die and remove this heavy body garment, you move to a stage which is very similar to us as regards motion, formation and relationship, especially at the lower stages of your non-material existence, when you shall live in a parallel world very similar to your world as regards places and feelings. Your physical, sensory life is but a school in which you learn, taste, hear, smell and see, and you graduate after death to a non-material world, a feelings world. You benefit from your earlier life by acquiring certain experiences that qualify you for the non-material life, and you become capable of certain conceptualisations through which you live and develop to higher and higher grades. You repeat the experience over and over again. Each time the experiences increase greatly, to reach the final form that promotes you to a higher plane. What I want to say is that you are similar to us in that first stage of the other world.*

Q   If I ever became like you, what would I see?

A   *You would see a transparent, misty life. No matter binds us, no physics or chemistry, but feelings and formations similar to you in appearance, i.e., general appearances, but as to the contents, we differ much from you.*

Q   Do you eat and drink, or what are your energy sources?

A   *We do not eat or drink. We are energies by ourselves. Programmed energies subject to higher law, we develop or degrade as per our deeds. We are also subject to the law of [divine] reward and penalty like you. Our good deeds reflect positively, providing us with the subtlety that promotes us on up the staircase of transcendence, and our evil deeds make us go back towards higher density and keep us within the bottom layers.*

Q   Why are you called inhabitants of lower-order worlds, despite the fact that you—especially the believers among you—have, as I understand it, a composition similar to angels?

A   *We've been described by this term [lower order] for an important reason. The reason is not our position [in the universe], as some would think; it is because we are below you in density. As I said before, it is a reversed staircase for us, but for you the staircase is not reversed, and here lies the secret: Had this staircase been not reversed, the jinn would have been humans in advanced stages, i.e., transcending the material state, thus becoming angels, as you said.*

Q Am I to understand that when you develop, and are promoted, you go
   down, or is it the opposite?

A *Not spatially, as you understand it. You humans are very much bound by
   matter, in addition to time and space. The gist here is that we as jinn and you
   as humans have free will, the ability to choose good or evil, and this is what
   distinguishes us both. But each [of the two species] has its direction—not
   spatially, as you imagine, but mentally: we develop in a certain direction and
   you develop in an opposite direction. We live the first stage as neighbours, and
   talk to each other, as if we are undergoing an examination in the same school,
   but each in his own class. And at the end of this test, each of us exits through a
   separate door. We and you are a basic condition for the existence of this school,
   and while we are similar to you at one stage of your transitional stages,
   this does not mean that we mix with you after evolving.*

Q Many times I've heard about or seen human males or females possessed
   by jinn who go into convulsions and break down psychologically. This leads
   people to claim that all those who have relations with you are mentally ill,
   especially in the first stages. Can you explain this?

A *Can you imagine a watermelon entering you through your nostril? What
   torture that would be! It isn't easy for a foreign body to enter into the structure
   of another body. The torture affects both parties, the host and the hosted, but in
   different degrees. The jinn has a different consciousness, mind and environment,
   etc., and enters a body that's not parallel in structure, and this is what causes
   torture and misery, especially in the first stages.*

Q Then why do you enter these bodies?

A *For us, these bodies are a window of relief. The jinn who enters a human is
   fortunate and enjoys beautiful periods of his life, giving much of his time and
   energies in the service of humans . . .*

Q Why do cases of jinn manifestation or possession occur so frequently
   in our regions, or, to use a better phrase, in underdeveloped societies?
   Why not in America or Europe, for example?

A *There are possession cases all over the world, but their treatment differs from
   one region to another. In addition, we have a greater presence in certain
   societies because of the prevailing manner of thinking or the cultural
   background which provides the right setting for our entrances. As I said before,
   we wait for the proper moment and these are many among you. Also, you
   enrich the opportunity greatly, since your social composition is more suitable.*

Where are the Shadow People from?

Accounts of the jinn through the ages tell us that they are from a parallel world. In some occult circles, they are referred to as "ultraterrestrials," since they seem to enter our world from *within*. It is very clear that they are able to change their form and penetrate dense physical substances in a way that human beings cannot. Although Alice A. Bailey in her extensive works consciously avoids going into detail on beings of the nature of the jinn, she does cryptically refer to "visible" and "invisible" planets and planets that "veil" other planets. These are possibly the parallel worlds that are currently outside humanity's frame of reference.

In his "Essay on the Jinn (Demons),"[4] Ibn Taymiyah says:

> *Mankind should realize that Allah, the Exalted, the Almighty send [sic] Mohammad to both worlds; the world of man and the world of the Jinn. Belief in God and obedience to Him was made compulsory on the inhabitants of both worlds.*
>
> . . .
>
> *The Jinn are beings created with free will, living on earth in a world parallel to that of man, and are invisible to human eyes in their normal state. The Arabic word Jinn comes from the verb "Janna" which means to hide. . . . The term Jinni (Eng. Genie) is equivalent to Jinn. . . . In Islamic literature Shaytan (Eng. Satan, devil) is a name given to disbelieving Jinns. . . . They are created from fire according to Allah's statement in the Qur'an: The Jinns were created from the fire of a scorching wind. (Qur'an 15:27). They are not "fallen angels," as angels are made from light according to the following statement of Prophet Muhammad (bpuh) narrated by his wife 'A'ishah: "The angels were created from light and the Jinn from a fiery wind."*

Ibn Taymiyah tells us that the religion of Islam was introduced to the jinn in a similar way that it was introduced to humanity. Since the main objective of religion is to prepare the majority of human beings for a deeper understanding of spiritual growth, it makes sense that religion would also have been introduced to the jinn, perhaps through their relationships with human beings.

Since the jinn are a function of the notion of cosmic evil, as I explained in chapter 6, they are operating under the influence of a different, separative evolutionary law. In that system, the jinn are focused on developing the personality, and they function according to the principles of matter. That doesn't mean that they are inherently evil (although many of them are destructive); it simply means that they are from a system that has not yet evolved to the point that humanity has evolved, albeit that they clearly have different "equipment."

According to many Islamic texts, the jinn are envious of mankind since they were exiled from Earth to "a dry land." It is therefore possible that at some point in the extremely distant past, the jinn lived on Earth during a more separative evolutionary cycle but were not able to reach a point of evolution that would allow them to incarnate on Earth in the same way as human souls, and so they were exiled to a desolate parallel world, forcing them to enter the earth planes principally as fugitives.

It is important to bear in mind that the jinns' relative (in comparison to human beings) absence of spiritual growth means that even the more neutral among them lack the good conscience, judgment, and temperate nature of more evolved human beings. They can be vindictive, deceptive, capricious, volatile, and prone to undue harshness. By default, this makes them dangerous to interact with.

The evolutionary difference between humanity and the jinn inevitably gives rise to conflict and stems fundamentally from the conflict between the planetary deities who are respectively in charge of Earth and the parallel world of the jinn. It is precisely this conflict that has given rise to an apparent systemic weakness that allows the jinn to enter the earth planes at their convenience, running roughshod over humanity's free will and apparently invading our privacy at will.

The jinns' abilities have unsettling consequences for humanity; on the one end of the spectrum, privacy is easily infringed upon. Human beings are susceptible to disturbing jinn manifestations, and psychic mediums may be manipulated by the jinn to provide false information to their clients (all of these phenomena have been extensively documented). On the other end of the spectrum, humans may be led to destruction for sport or by way of retribution or out of spite. Of more concern is the risk of humans going backward in the evolutionary spectrum through association with the jinn, who may, consciously or unconsciously, interfere with humanity's connection to Spirit by pulling humans ever closer to matter and the baser instincts of the jinn evolutionary paradigm. In serious cases of possession, the ego part of the human soul may become detached from the personality, causing significant and long-lasting setbacks in the evolution of the soul.

Humanity will not help itself in overcoming this threat by complacency or by ignorance. Until a third, reconciling planetary god intervenes in this conflict to balance spirit and matter, Earth will continue to be visible and accessible by lower beings.

For those reasons, it is critical that human beings are aware of the jinn and know how to manage jinn encounters effectively. The starting point is being able to recognize the signs of jinn obsession when they begin to manifest to avoid full-blown possession, which is far more difficult to deal with.

OBSESSION

The obsession stage is one in which the more typical symptoms of so-called paranormal activity tend to manifest themselves. The objective of the jinn at this stage is to invade the human being's space and manipulate the human being, systematically destroying their willpower, thereby facilitating possession.

Such manipulation may be carried out through an attempt to strike up a relationship of some kind with the human being (paranormal sexual encounters, involving so-called succubi and incubi, are a common feature of this occurrence). Or—more commonly—the jinn may simply begin to terrorize the human being to instill fear and break down the human's resilience. The point of entry is the astral body of the human, or the desire center, which is why strong emotions such as fear feed obsession and must be actively controlled where obsession is suspected.

There are many documented accounts of the jinn choosing to frequent remote or abandoned places such as deserts and caves, but they are also present wherever human beings are, often becoming active around twilight and in the dark, perhaps because darkness is more conducive to shape-shifting and concealment on the basis of jinn anatomy.

Jinn are also able to enter the dreams of human beings in some circumstances, as is apparent in the phenomenon of sleep paralysis, in which frightening beings invade the human's dreams—apparently with the specific intention of intimidating them.

Another interesting trend recently circulating on TikTok involves dreamers asking beings in their dreams for the date and time. The response from these beings is always hostile and seems to be deliberately designed to cultivate fear—the dreamscape takes a turn for the worse, and dreamers are told that they are not allowed to ask such questions. This is without doubt a mechanism for the jinn to obsess and possess human beings on an enormous scale as thousands of people—usually young people—participate in what they think is a fun game, unwittingly exposing themselves to danger of obsession and possession, and undoubtedly contributing to a destructive, fear-based thought form that preys on those who are asleep.

Human beings often unwittingly play into jinn encounters in other ways by deliberately using occult tools such as Ouija boards to call on "spirits" for amusement or out of morbid curiosity. In the absence of appropriate boundaries and strategic intention, dialing into the jinn is very likely to yield unpleasant consequences. Using these tools in ignorance is an invitation to the jinn to obsess human beings, creating portals for the jinn to easily enter human space and—if they are so inclined—stick around and cause problems.

As I explained in chapter 1, where there is etheric body dysfunction in the form of a loose connection between a human being's dense physical body and their etheric physical body, this makes them more susceptible to obsession and possession. This type of dysfunction can relatively easily arise through shock, trauma, and physical injury and means that individuals who dabble in the occult in ignorance may also be unaware that they are more susceptible than others to problems with jinn.

Apart from exercising sound judgment when it comes to jinn encounters, it is also a good idea to maintain a regime suitable for maintaining etheric body resilience, including through physical training to strengthen the physical body, and energy-based modalities such as yoga, tai chi, chi gung, nei gung, Eastern acupuncture, or sound-healing sessions, or a combination of these.

Turning to the symptoms of the obsession phase, there may be flickering lights or lights that turn themselves on or off in the absence of any human interaction, inexplicable cold breezes or cold "patches" in rooms, or strange rumblings in a building that are not attributable to any logical cause (so-called astral knockings). Doors may slam unprovoked, or there may be unpleasant smells, disturbed sleep or insomnia, or unusual fixation on sexual activity. There may be light or dark presences at the periphery of one's vision or—more rarely—in plain sight, unshakeable feelings of unease, and a sense that one is being watched. The immune system may also weaken.

In summary, symptoms of obsession can include:

- flickering lights or other electricity-related issues

- feelings of unease or anxiety and sudden fear of the darkness

- feelings of being watched

- persistent feelings that something is "off"

- physical or psychic sightings of diabolical or monstrous beings, which may appear in various forms, from dark, featureless masses to humanoid beings with flaws, such as opaque eyes (red eyes are also common)

- moving or translocation of objects

- inexplicable cold breezes or "patches"

- unpleasant or strange odors that are impossible to get rid of

- strange noises, such as slamming doors, when it is apparent that no doors have actually slammed

- headaches that persist for more than a few days and that may be unresponsive to painkillers

- persistent insomnia

- a depressed immune system

- nightmares

- sleep paralysis

- difficulty remembering or focusing on protective measures or rituals

In some cases, the jinn may strategically possess animals, such as cats, to get closer to human beings, observe them, and then obsess them. When a domestic animal has been possessed, the eyes will look different and there may be an accompanying sense of the presence of something sinister. It is important to be mindful of the fact that the animal itself is innocent in these cases.

On the other hand, cats are often the first to detect the presence of a jinn, since they are able to see phenomena that human beings aren't able to see. I once had a cat who was extremely adept at identifying jinn—he seemed to know that they were dangerous, and he would warn me of their presence. I would see him looking around the room suspiciously and then growling threateningly. He never growled in other circumstances.

Obsession commonly manifests itself in acrimony in relationships where there is apparently no other reason for any conflict. The victims of obsession may become uncharacteristically moody or aggressive or begin to turn on each other. Electricity and water sources (such as televisions and bathrooms) are common entry or focal points, as are mirrors, dolls, figurines, statues, and images of people and deities, which should be avoided and covered up where obsession is suspected.

Churches and other sanctified places are far from immune to paranormal activity; in fact, they are often particularly susceptible to infestation (owing, for example, to their historical construction in places of concentrated energy or the presence of graveyards, which are usually rife with jinn).

A common mistake on the part of human beings is to assume that orbs of light and other apparently innocuous paranormal phenomena are necessarily angelic in nature. Unfortunately, the deceptive nature of the jinn means that they are apt to masquerade as helpful devas, such as guardian angels.

New Age–type material such as books, workshops, and information on social media that relates to angels, orbs, and other so-called beings of light must always be consumed advisedly; in other words, by recognizing the risk of deception and of encountering destructive or—at the very least—untrustworthy beings.

The jinn don't care how spiritual or compassionate you are or whether you have a certificate in angel therapy. Nor do they care whether you believe in the occult or the paranormal. If you are human and they gain access to your environment, they will, if they are minded to, seek to manipulate or destroy you—or use you to destroy others. If you are making yourself visible on the subtle planes by meditating or astral travel, or by practicing Reiki or ceremonial magic or any other kind of magic (whether or not you believe that it truly is "magic"), or by reading astrological charts or by divination, then you had better make sure that you can competently intercept and, if necessary, dispose of destructive forces.

When you are dealing with a destructive jinn, it is unrealistic to exclusively rely on traditional New Age paraphernalia such as crystals and sage. Although they are effective for certain types of clearing and healing, they are inadequate when it comes to dealing with obsession. For those of you who are familiar with banishing rituals, such as the Lesser Banishing Ritual of the Pentagram, they have in my experience tended to offer variable levels of success. While they can be helpful, in some cases, they cannot be exclusively relied upon. When a jinn is actively working to harass, terrorize, and break down the will of the human target, exorcism may be the only workable solution.

If you are an adept who is actively working in service, or you begin to pay a lot of focused attention to the jinn, such as through writing or study, you will be far more visible to the jinn, and destructive beings will be doubly intent on undermining your efforts. That may make you more susceptible to obsession than most and means that it is even more important that you maintain effective spiritual hygiene and cultivate energetic boundaries and support systems by staying on the path of light (or evolution), regularly invoking the assistance of guardian angels and, where you have the appropriate skill set, other helpful devas.

POSSESSION

Possession occurs when one or more jinns gain entry to the human soul, having been given express or implied permission to do so. In those circumstances, the human has two options: to muster all their willpower and energy reserves to exorcise the jinn and break the energetic link or, in more serious cases, sooner or later to die or suffer significant damage at the level of the path of evolution as a result of the possession.

Express permission may be given where, for example, a human undertakes a ritual to bind themselves to a jinn (classically referred to as selling one's soul) in return for material gain of some kind or where they deliberately invoke a jinn through ritual. The gravity of such workings should not be underestimated. If a ritual is effectively undertaken with the appropriate intent, there will be consequences. Sometimes those consequences are irreversible.

Implied permission is a more nebulous and unsettling notion. The jinn, which may already be present in the human's environment, will systematically and obsessively break down the human will until the human gives up all resistance. Or the human may implicitly invite the jinn in; for example, through sympathetic magic, where there is consistent use of infernal symbols (the archetypes of form or matter) such as the inverted pentagram, or a strong identification with diabolical forces. Where obsession or possession is suspected, my strong advice is to get rid of any symbols that are attuned (whether or not deliberately) to diabolical forces.

Depending on how far the situation has progressed, symptoms of possession can include the following:

- A noticeable change in appearance for the worse or black or opaque eyes— eyes are usually a dead giveaway.

- Blinking, heart palpitations, shaking, or convulsing—the adrenal system seems to be unconsciously impacted during possession.

- Persistent feelings or projections of anger or hostility

- Antisocial or odd behavior

- Unusual physical weakness or a lack of energy (or both)

- A sense of separation

- A lack of appetite

- Unusually hostile responses from people around the victim—they may take an instant disliking to the victim.

- A tendency to attract combative situations with unusual frequency

- An apparent lack of humanity

- Feelings of revulsion toward traditional symbols of Spirit (such as ecclesiastical tools) and recitations from holy texts

- Unpleasant body odor

- A decline in the physical body

ADDRESSING OBSESSION AND POSSESSION

It is obvious that many of the symptoms associated with obsession and possession also apply to conditions, such as medical conditions, which may be completely unrelated to the paranormal. Discernment is therefore key, and it may be necessary to call on healthcare and medical professionals to rule out, for example, mental illness.

If common sense is applied, and the principles that I have outlined above are effectively followed, such as cultivating an effective spiritual support network by cultivating a connection to Spirit rather than by practicing black magic through the devas of form, most encounters with jinn can be headed off at the obsession stage.

If possession occurs, and the victim does not have the necessary skills to help themselves, help must be sought out from someone who specializes in exorcism and is truly adept in the practice, and *not* someone who only half believes in what they are doing and simply goes through the motions.

While a comprehensive guide on the practice of exorcism is outside the scope of this book, it may be helpful to draw from one or more of the following methods, most of which I can vouch for on the basis of my own experiences:

■ Take immediate steps to calm strong and unruly emotions, such as fear, which allow the jinn to gain a stronger foothold, thereby exposing the person to a greater risk of possession.

■ Command the jinn to leave (e.g., the room/person) in the name of Spirit (whatever form your particular connection to Spirit or Divinity may take). This is an assertion of self-autonomy and free will under the protection of the Divine and must be executed unequivocally and with complete confidence.

■ Recitation of the rites of exorcism or other holy exhortations. It isn't difficult to get hold of the rites of exorcism with which you may have some spiritual affinity; for example, through practicing a particular religion or being christened or baptized under the auspices of that religion. As I have discussed elsewhere in this book, intoning a word is an act of creation, and the power of the word to dispel or expel unwanted presences should not be underestimated, however bonkers it may seem to the inexperienced, particularly when there is a long lineage of spiritually connected authorities behind the use of a particular passage. The Psalms in the Christian Bible, such as Psalm 121 (to keep unwanted presences at bay), are particularly potent.

■ Salt and specialized herbal baths. Salt has long been known for its cleansing properties—it is a powerful agent in removing unwanted attachments of all kinds (or the residue of them). It follows that holy water—a combination of consecrated salt and water—is a powerful remedy. It is possible to purchase ready-made holy water from hoodoo or voodoo botanicas and some New

Age shops if you do not have the skills to make it yourself. Special herbal remedies to remove attachments, for clearing purposes and the like, can also be purchased from botanicas—or you can make them yourself.

- Playing classical music or music with a connection to Divinity in a room for a couple of hours, at least, where a presence is detected. This method is probably a book in and of itself, but I have found the holy names and the "om" frequency to be particularly potent.

- Sound healing, such as Acutonics, and the use of overtones. In this context, I specifically deal with the Hygiea asteroid frequency in chapter 7. Your Acutonics or other sound practitioner will be able to administer the appropriate sound frequencies according to your particular circumstances.

- Singing holy songs such as "Dona Nobis Pacem" ("Grant Us Peace") or intoning mantras

- Talismans, such as the Hexagram of Solomon. These are useful when they are worn on a limited basis.

- Avoiding horror movies

- Throwing away any paraphernalia associated with destructive beings (such as demonic imagery), since they are powerful amplifiers of that type of energy, and energetic links to the jinn must be broken to exorcise it.

- Protecting the back of the skull around the area of the occipital lobe (the entry point for possession) when obsession is suspected, by covering that area with consecrated garments. Assuming that you are not able to get hold of a consecrated garment such as a priest's stole, you will need to make one yourself, using relevant holy imagery and consecrating it yourself, should you have the appropriate skills.

- Subject to what I outline above regarding overreliance on crystals and banishing rituals; these can be helpful in establishing protective energetic boundaries—ideally as a prevention rather than as a cure. Jade, obsidian, black tourmaline, turquoise, smoky quartz, tiger's eye, and labradorite all are useful crystals in that regard.

- Syrian rue. This is a powerful jinn deterrent, and I take it in homeopathic form. I make a point of taking it with me when I travel. Since I am not a medical professional, please obtain professional medical advice before you consider ingesting this herb in any form.

- Mandrake roots. These are traditionally hung above the front door of a house to protect its occupants.

- Iron (for example, in the form of lodestone) and silver have been written about through the ages as effective deterrents against the jinn. I have also found copper (for example, in the form of copper bracelets) to be a highly effective jinn deterrent. The efficacy of metals in protecting against jinn possession comes from their connection to particular planets that embody particular archetypes.

- Wearing or displaying meaningful sacred symbols; in particular, symbols that have been consecrated or powerfully linked to Divinity, such as holy texts.

- Chinese Five Element acupuncture (administered by a qualified professional). I have found this to be of invaluable assistance over the years. Acupuncturists are taught (or have access to) specific exorcism protocols.

- Avoiding discussions about the jinn with other people through electronic devices such as mobile phones. The jinn have a particular affinity with electricity and can reach other people through electronic devices.

THE JINN OF THE APPALACHIAN MOUNTAINS

I want to make particular mention of the jinn concentration in the Appalachian Mountains in northeastern North America, since they will not respond to some of the general methods that I have outlined above.

The Appalachian phenomenon is attracting a lot of attention on TikTok, which is unhelpfully fueling fear of these jinns, allowing them, perversely, to get a firmer foothold on humanity through the electricity and thought forms generated by social media, and by increasing tourism to the Appalachian Mountains.

The Appalachian jinn are an ancient abomination, again rooted in cosmic "evil," and they are especially envious of human beings. Their presence on Earth was perpetuated in part by foolish behavior on the part of humanity many ages ago. I do not currently have more detail in that regard.

Actively seeking the destruction of humans, they whistle and call people by name, and they have a peculiar ability to manifest in physical form, often with red eyes.

Once the fear around these jinn subsides, so too will their destructive capabilities. It is therefore important that we avoid sensationalizing them and stirring up fear-based intrigue by way of social media.

Although the Appalachian jinn will not respond as readily to traditional exorcism, the playing of sacred sounds is helpful, and it is important to energetically protect the borders of any property in the Appalachians to prevent them from encroaching on homes. They must not be engaged with or listened to, since they are adepts at manipulation by way of sound.

SOME OF MY OWN ENCOUNTERS WITH THE JINN

What follows is an account of some of my own experiences of obsession and possession, peppered variously with naivety, hubris, misjudgment, and initial reluctance to take responsibility because I didn't "feel like" having to deal with the jinn. I hope that you will use these accounts to succeed where I have fallen short.

Obsession

In 2013, my husband and I were invited for dinner with some friends in a village in South West England. They had been living in the house for only a few months, and this would be our first opportunity to see their new home. They had invited us to stay the night so that we wouldn't need to drive back to my own home after midnight, but I felt strangely uncomfortable at the prospect of staying over, so we planned to drive straight home afterward.

We arrived at around 7 p.m., just in time to be given a tour of the house and to greet our friends' three very young children before they were put to bed. I immediately disliked the "feeling" of the house.

After the children had been put to bed, the adults sat down to eat at the dining-room table. I had a single alcoholic drink when the starters were served, and nothing else after that. As the evening progressed, I began to feel inexplicably depressed and alienated, despite the company. I should note that I am not an emotional person, nor am I susceptible to depression or other types of mental illness, and I wasn't on any kind of medication.

After a while, I left the table and headed for the toilet in the hallway. A sense of unease descended on me, and my feelings of separation and misery deepened. I entered the toilet and locked the door. Up to that point, I had made no connection with the possibility of paranormal activity. As I tried to work out why I suddenly felt so alienated and depressed, I noticed a movement at the corner of my right eye. As I turned my head and watched, incredulous, the door handle began to move slowly downward. All was silent; no noises were coming from outside the toilet, and I couldn't hear the rest of the party in the dining room. Using a holy imperative, I mentally commanded whatever it was that was moving the door handle to leave me. The door handle immediately returned to its starting point. The silence remained unbroken.

I quickly left the toilet and returned to the dining room, taking steps to protect myself energetically. For the rest of the evening, I was on high alert and the feeling of depression abated, although I continued to feel unsettled in the house.

Just before midnight, the party decamped to a large conservatory without curtains on the windows along three walls. Since the house was in the countryside, not a single light was visible in the darkness beyond the windows. I felt a sense of foreboding. Sure enough, within minutes I saw the shape of an unrecognizable figure reflected in the windows. I reinforced my efforts to protect myself energetically, and my husband and I went home shortly afterward.

Possession

During a trip to Prague in the former Czech Republic, my husband and I stayed in a beautiful, quaint, sixteenth-century hotel in Prague's Mala Strana (or Lesser Town), one of Prague's most historic regions.

When I read up on the hotel before my trip, I was immediately wary of its age and felt slightly unsettled by the photographs of the antique furniture in the rooms; I wanted a peaceful holiday, undisturbed by the paranormal.

My internal defense mechanisms began to kick in properly a few days before the trip. I felt compelled to take a salt bath infused with protective herbs. I also decided to wear my Hexagram of Solomon pendant, which I usually use only at times when I strongly suspect that I am under attack.

In the early hours of the morning on which we were due to leave London for Prague, I had a disturbing dream. I was in a "Mafia" house, waiting for the "Mafia" owner to return, and I was beset with feelings of apprehension. In the dream I saw the owner as a cruel and ruthless man with an olive complexion and dark hair. I found myself looking for a bathroom in the house but instead walked into what appeared to be a hospital room with rows of beds.

I awoke from the dream convinced that I was being shown my hotel in Prague. I was puzzled by the "Mafia" reference and assumed that the house had been involved in some kind of Czech black-market activity—perhaps during the former Communist regime. I was also intrigued by the "hospital" room. I decided to try to investigate the history of the house as far as possible upon my arrival.

Unfortunately, my subtle questioning of the house's current owners and staff yielded frustratingly anodyne responses. I assumed that they were deliberately avoiding going into detail about the house's history, in view of the tangible sensitivity around Prague's Communist past. There was no mention of underhanded dealings or hospitals.

I felt uncomfortable in our room from the moment that I stepped over the threshold, despite the outward charm of the room. It consisted of a dressing and bathroom area, as well as a separate bedroom. Something told me that I would need to carry out regular banishings in both rooms.

That night, I felt genuinely scared to walk from my bed to the toilet in the dark. I had also come down with a cold and struggled to sleep. Feelings of being watched, insomnia, and a depressed immune system—especially when experienced simultaneously—all are classic warning signs of obsession, which I did not take seriously enough at the time. I hoped that I could simply keep undesirable presences at bay by carrying out the occasional banishing ritual. That was a mistake.

For the first two days, I wore the Hexagram of Solomon on a chain, day and night, and carried out banishing rituals once a day at twilight, when my feelings of unease in the room began to deepen. After the second night, I decided that it was safe to remove the Hexagram of Solomon since I felt physically uncomfortable sleeping with it on. At that point, the possibility of jinn interference still hadn't consciously entered my mind. In hindsight, I can now see that it was precisely at the point that I removed the Hexagram of Solomon that the paranormal activity had taken a turn for the worse. I had been stripped of my protective buffer—my tangible link to Spirit—and was now pretty much a sitting duck for energetic breach.

The house had a cellar, which was being used as a recreational area by hotel residents. The cellar's historical access point from outside the front of the house had been bricked up but was still visible from inside the cellar. One night, a group of hotel residents gathered in the cellar for a tour-related discussion. My husband and I were among the first to arrive, and we pulled out chairs in front of the bricked-up cellar access point. As I sat down, I immediately felt a wave of negative energy emanating from the bricked-up area. I moved to a different position at the table.

The next day, on a tour of the area around the hotel, our tour guide pointed out a statue of Saint Procopius of Sazava, the eleventh-century patron saint of Bohemia. The statue was set into the front facade of a historical house and featured Saint Procopius holding a scepter in his right hand and a chain in his left hand. A devil was attached to the chain. Our tour guide explained that Saint Procopius had been a well-known exorcist.

Sensing that the statue was significant, and for purposes relating to my spiritual work, I decided to take a photograph of it. I focused my phone camera on the statue and tapped the screen to take the photo, but for no apparent reason my phone camera button jammed, and when I looked at my phone, I saw that my camera had already taken 115 photos of the devil, blocking out all but Saint Procopius's feet. My attempts to stop my phone taking incessant photos of the devil and the feet of the statute were initially futile—I couldn't even switch the phone off. Eventually, I walked about 50 meters away from the statute, and, having addressed what I realized was a jinn directly, exhorting it to leave, I was finally able to resolve the technical issues. It became clear to me at that point that I was being obsessed.

Back in the hotel later that afternoon, while lying on the bed in our room, I saw a diminutive skeleton hovering a little way away from me, beneath the ceiling. The skeleton seemed childlike and had long, blonde hair. The apparition disappeared almost immediately.

The banishing ritual that I performed at dusk later that day was revealing. As I began to weave the familiar energetic lines that vibrated in the air and intoned the necessary words, I noticed what appeared to be a swarm of opaque, white, feather-like objects rush past me from the right. I knew that I was dealing with something or—more likely—some *things* far more dangerous than the ghost of a dead human being.

The next day, during an afternoon nap, I had a disturbing dream. In my dream, I was alone in the house and heard the unmistakable sounds of a grave being dug outside, of shovel against stone. I was filled with terror in my dream as I realized that there was no obvious explanation for the sounds and that they were paranormal in origin—I was being shown a fragment of a past event.

On awakening, I carried out a divination using Tarot cards to try to work out what I was being shown. The cards suggested that children had been buried somewhere in or near the house; they also suggested that a woman—perhaps a servant and mistress of one of the house's former occupants—had been murdered and buried in the vicinity after becoming pregnant with an unwanted child.

Later that day, during a function attended by one of our tour guides, I asked our guide whether she had any knowledge of the house. She told me that the house backed onto an area that had become heavily occupied by Italians in the sixteenth century and that at some point it had been a hospital. She also mentioned that it was near an orphanage and—she understood—a mass children's grave. Her explanation backed up my dream vision of the hospital and may have accounted for the "Mafia" references in my first dream. Perhaps one of the house's former occupants had been Italian or had been involved in Italian black-market activity in the area.

The references to the orphanage and the mass grave were also illuminating, given my sighting of the childlike skeleton, my dream of grave digging, and the card reading.

I indicated that I had experienced some paranormal activity in the house, and the tour guide told me that the house had been built in an area that had "very powerful energy" and was an ancient pagan worship site.

By my last night in the hotel, the paranormal influences had escalated to a crisis point. Yet, for some unknown reason—most likely because I was to some extent still under their influence, although I should have known better—I was still reluctant to carry out an exorcism. As I walked into our hotel room after dinner, the words of an ancient canonical song filled my mind: "Dona Nobis Pacem." The words, meaning "Grant us peace," come from the Latin Mass or the liturgy of the Roman Catholic Mass in Latin.

I was taught "Dona Nobis Pacem" when I was about eleven years old, as a member of my school's choir. Although I had not thought about the song for a long time, I began to sing it out loud as I entered my hotel room that night.

I performed a further banishing ritual and took a homeopathic remedy before I went to bed, as a block against further attack. I was acutely aware of the need to layer on as much protection as possible.

Needless to say, I barely slept that night. As I tossed and turned, the words "Dona Nobis Pacem" ran incessantly through my mind to ward off the looming presence of something deeply destructive. The left-hand side of my face felt as though it was burning up with fever. Between wakefulness and restless sleep, I had visions of a black hole of a grave supported on its periphery by wooden planks, which I dared not look into, and what I can describe only as a bull-like deity—its face full of cruelty—carved in stone.

In the early hours of the next morning, I waited for dawn and my imminent departure from the hotel. As I listened to the familiar creaking from a corner of the ceiling, it occurred to me that there was no rational explanation for the sound. The guests staying in the room above were clearly not walking around (or I would have heard their heavy footsteps), and I was lying in my bed in a state of near paralysis. All was quiet in the house but for the creaking. My husband slept soundly, apparently unaware.

Waiting for the plane to take off later that day on our return to London, I mused over the bull-like deity that had appeared to me in vision during the night. I wondered how it was connected to the house's past, the children, and the mass grave. Some cursory research revealed that the stone deity in my vision appeared to have similar features to Moloch, a "demon" worshiped by the Ammonites (a biblical tribe ostensibly associated with the Israelites), who had made sacrifices of children to "him."

Although the tour guide had spoken of an ancient pagan worship site in the vicinity of the hotel, and the deity in my vision had borne similar features to Moloch, I can only speculate as to whether the hotel had indeed been on the site of child sacrifice to a demonic being. On the other hand, that explanation seems credible, given my dreams and visions. And the fact that there had been an orphanage and a mass children's grave at the back of the house seems to be more than mere coincidence. It seemed to me that the area was fraught with the misery and despair of its ever-changing populace, presided over by an entity that had been actively fueled by its form—worshiping human subjects.

At home in London, it took considerable effort on my part over the next few days to rid myself entirely of the jinn, including herbal baths and rituals involving recitation of the Psalms and other holy texts.

I once had an opportunity to stay at an English university residence in a city in southern England for just under a week during the summer. I had asked for a "quiet room" and had been duly allocated room number 10 at the very top of staircase 11.

Staircase 11 was directly opposite the college chapel.

From the moment I entered my room, I felt uneasy; it smelled odd, and although it was clean, it "felt" dirty to me. Yet, I consciously pushed my reservations to one side since the very last thing I felt like doing was engaging with what I assumed to be a ghost. I also quashed a nagging feeling that I should carry out the Lesser Banishing Ritual of the Pentagram. I did, however, put together a makeshift altar in the sitting area for the specific purposes of protection. This would prove to be a completely ineffective measure—not least because I failed to properly engage with it.

Over the first few days of my stay at the college, my vague feelings of uneasiness evolved into an increasing awareness of something hostile, the bluntest indication of which was an incredibly bright fluorescent white light that kept switching itself on in my en suite bathroom. There was no apparent source for this light, since I could see one lightbulb over the mirror (which remained switched off), and the only other lights in the bathroom were a very dim, yellow light in the shower and a green smoke detector light in the doorway. More disturbing still, the fluorescent white light switched itself on every night at precisely 11:35 p.m.—and occasionally at other times (notably one morning at 7:35 a.m., just after my alarm clock had gone off). I began to feel distressed by the paranormal activity but obstinately refused to engage with it.

On the second night, I was just drifting off to sleep when my bedroom was again flooded with florescent white light emanating from the bathroom. I looked at the digital clock on my mobile phone. It was 11:35 p.m. At that point, I felt that I had no choice but to engage with the being. Unfortunately, I made a fatal error of judgment.

Taking into account the age and history of the building (which was first built in the fourteenth century), I assumed that the being was merely a ghost refusing to leave the physical plane. I decided to go into vision and encourage the being to cross over to "the other side." So, shortly before midnight that night, in the absence of any divination to ascertain the cause of the disturbances, I sat cross-legged on the floor of the sitting room that adjoined my bedroom. Needless to say, I used no protective circle, tool, or talisman; fortunately, I had the presence of mind to evoke certain helpful devas who warned me to take additional protective steps.

What I encountered in vision was a collection of evil-looking beings, one of which appeared to be a woman dressed in Victorian night clothing, "grinning strangely," as my journal records. I immediately noticed that something wasn't quite right with her eyes.

The jinn will commonly appear in human form to deceive or confuse, but their presence will be marred by a defect of some kind. Such flaws will often manifest in the eyes, which may, for example, appear completely black. Similarly, those who are possessed will exhibit physical symptoms of such defects, including opaque "black" eyes and unusual pallor.

Returning to the woman in the Victorian night clothing, upon sighting this being I made my second error of judgment that night by assuming that "she" must be the ghost of a deceased human being, trapped on the astral plane and possessed by a jinn. To my mind, the logical next step would simply be to remove the jinn and then release the ghost to the mental plane. In hindsight, I strongly suspect that the woman was a jinn masquerading as a ghost. That mistake made me highly susceptible to possession—with no real boundaries in place, I had effectively given the jinn permission to step right into me.

The possession manifested itself in a very physical way in this case—I experienced heart palpitations of a magnitude that I had never had before and never have since (which was in and of itself terrifying) and uncontrollably blinking eyelids. My adrenal system went into overdrive. All of this had happened in the absence of any fear—bear in mind that for all intents and purposes, I thought that I was merely escorting a ghost to "the other side." Up until that point, I had been comfortable with the operation. Too comfortable. It was, in fact, my adrenal response that had alerted me to the danger. Only then did it occur to me that I was dealing with a jinn. Had it not been for the additional protective measures that I had been encouraged to take as I embarked on the ritual, I suspect that the possession would have been far worse. Although the jinn had gained access to my physical body, the magical barriers that I had put in place with devic assistance meant that I was afforded a level of protection.

In the ensuing days, the symptoms of paranormal activity continued to escalate. I suffered from insomnia and became increasingly moody and reclusive, choosing to avoid eating in the dining room in favor of eating meals in my room. I spent almost all my spare time in my room, effectively allowing the jinn free rein.

That type of behavior is significant in that victims of obsession and possession typically begin to lose their ability to exercise sound judgment and become increasingly subject to the jinn's control. Logic dictates that, knowing what I did at the time, I should have avoided being in my room at all costs and that I should have sought to be moved to another room. Perversely, I was increasingly drawn to my room, despite the ongoing obsession and possession. Even when the porter told me that there had been reports of significant paranormal activity at the college, notably in the chapel (which was directly opposite my room), I failed to ask him to move me out of my room. It simply didn't occur to me.

As the week wore on, it felt increasingly as though I was wading through a thick mental fog—I found it difficult to focus on the problem at hand. I felt inexplicable cold breezes and saw things moving beyond my bed in the dark. I would be awoken by the undeniable presence of evil at night but would be too scared to open my eyes because I knew that what I would see with my physical sight would terrify me. One afternoon, while lying on my bed, I experienced another direct attack, which manifested as palpitations similar to the ones I had experienced before. I commanded the jinn to leave me, and the palpitations immediately subsided.

Toward the end of my stay, I had the distinct impression that the jinn was redoubling its efforts to break down my will, since I was still quite obviously resisting its presence. I would be woken up by loud knockings, which appeared to originate from somewhere above my head, as though an invisible hand were rapping on my window ledge. I began to see a hostile being when I closed my eyes at night, and the strange, florescent light would turn itself on more frequently.

On my last day, I returned to my room on staircase 11 to collect my bags, which involved making a few trips up and down the stairs. I made my last trip downstairs, fully intending to return to my room one last time to leave a tip for the cleaner, but I never returned because something told me to avoid going back into that room at all costs. Had I deceived the jinn? Would something awful have happened to me if I had returned to my room for the last time that day? I strongly suspect so.

Fortunately, I was able to overcome the possession on my own at home through herbal baths and rituals, in parallel with some very potent exorcism treatments by a Chinese Five Elements acupuncturist.

EXTRATERRESTRIALS

This chapter would not be complete without a passing reference to extraterrestrials or "aliens," since there appears to be significant crossover between the jinn and the other beings who invade our world (ostensibly in unidentified flying objects or "UFOs") to further apparently selfish agendas by using subterfuge, illusion, and coercion. These extraterrestrials must be distinguished from the powerful, benevolent extraplanetary devas that I refer to earlier in this chapter.

There are countless records of aliens abducting human beings with malevolent intent, in many cases unexpectedly, in circumstances in which it would appear to be futile to try to invoke traditional methods of clearing and exorcism. These beings are no doubt of a more powerful and dangerous nature than other jinn (and indeed it is quite conceivable that they may come from different parallel worlds, which are also adverse to the current evolutionary position of humanity). Recently there have been a slew of UFO sightings, leading to speculation about whether they are in fact extraterrestrial in origin or whether they are linked to human spy technology.

Robert Lebling says:[5]

Imagine a species of intelligent beings that live secretly among us. Imagine that they often appear humanoid or even human but possess amazing powers that we lack. They can change their shapes, can fly through the air[,] and can even render themselves invisible. They watch us, study us[,] and react to us. Occasionally they abduct humans and even mate with them, producing hybrid offspring. In today's

North America or Europe, such creatures are discussed in all seriousness by many—
they are called "aliens" or "Greys." In the Middle East, Africa[,] and Asia, beings
that fit this description are called "jinn."

...

In the case of so-called "alien" encounters, humanity is clearly once again on the wrong side of the conflict between planetary deities as they work out their evolutionary differences, and the beings who embody cosmic "evil" continue to interfere in the human system.

It is clearly important that we human beings cultivate awareness and undergo the necessary spiritual growth, continuing to focus on our own evolutionary path along the lines of the Law of Attraction and refining our connection to Spirit, rather than remaining fixated on external growth through matter or form and the personality, which is a relic from our previous evolutionary epoch.

The next stage in human evolution will entail developing the ability to combine matter and spirit. At that stage, the conflict between matter and spirit will be resolved through the intervention of a third, reconciling planetary deity, and cosmic "evil," as it currently manifests on Earth, will dissipate.

Our primary task as an evolving species is therefore to concentrate on reaching our evolutionary zenith at this time by cultivating the ability to cocreate with Spirit. As more and more human beings focus on perfecting internal growth (that is, from the perspective of the soul), the more rapidly humanity will make progress toward the next stage of its development, since human beings are the cogs in the machine driving the great planetary deity in its own evolutionary journey. The more we lean into our higher consciousness, the less susceptible we will be to extraterrestrial control.

GHOSTS

Spontaneously transported in vision again, I revisited another of my past incarnations. The only thing is that this time I wasn't *alive*.

I was with a significant other from an indefinite time in the past, in a place that felt frigid and bereft of vitality. Everything appeared in faded watercolors; every action seemed to be a pointless reflex.

We were teenagers in the Deep South of the United States, and we were in love. Yet, we were fixated on carrying out some kind of mechanistic ritual; we kept on visiting the same pool of water in the same woods over and over again. Sometimes we visited our respective childhood homes, which were just as miserable—they had no furnishings or occupants.

At last, after countless reenactments of these depressing scenes, it occurred to me to consciously ask myself why we kept getting into the water when it was so damn cold and uninviting.

The thought was a clarion call from my soul on the mental plane, calling back that part of my consciousness that had refused to move on after my childhood death.

I learned from my experience by assimilating it into my consciousness—that it is futile to hang around in the physical plane in perpetuity after the death of the dense physical body. And that it's futile to refuse to let go of the people you love once they've gone.

I was a ghost in denial: an astral shadow of a physical body from which I had long since withdrawn. Much like the moon, which continues to haunt the earth, drawing humanity toward matter and away from Spirit, even though she is long dead[1] and her influence is waning. Humanity continues to enact its rituals, following the cycles of the moon, in apparent conformity with a planetary ghost.

Changes will come as the moon slowly wastes away and her astral body eventually dissipates, but for now at least the pattern is evident in those human beings who, having experienced death, choose to delay their progress by remaining in astral form as ghosts or apparitions. (I am deliberately not referring to these entities as "discarnate" beings, since that term could refer to other kinds of beings who do not manifest in dense physical form in the same way as human beings do.)

The fascinating thing is that unlike the physical and mental planes, the astral plane is an illusory state of consciousness created by humanity, born of excessive emotion and the desires of the personality (as distinct from the cocreative, intelligent desire implicit in the Law of Attraction). If we recall from chapter 1 that the astral body is in effect the emotional body, and that a critical part of the work of the evolving human being is to develop the ability to gain control over their emotions so that they can experience them but not perpetuate an unbalanced emotional state, it becomes very clear that when humanity evolves to the point that their emotions no longer have any impact on them, the astral plane will disintegrate, becoming defunct. Until then, the astral body will continue to trap most human beings—whether they are alive or dead—hindering the evolution of their consciousness:

> *The sentient substance which constitutes the astral plane is still being gathered into forms of illusion and still forms a barrier in the path of the soul seeking liberation. It still "holds prisoner" the many people who die whilst their major reaction to life is that of desire, of wishful thinking and of emotional sentiency. These are still the vast majority.*[2]

...

Those human beings who have advanced to the point where they are no longer controlled by their emotions will not spend any time at all in the astral plane at the point of death; instead, they will go directly to the mental plane to prepare for their next incarnation. From that it follows that sightings of the deceased by the living are possible only in cases where the deceased have not yet mastered their emotions. This is because contact with the deceased on the mental plane would need to take place through the mental faculties.[3]

It is therefore obvious that we must consciously train ourselves, first, to manage our emotions appropriately, and second, to remember at the point of death that to remain in the astral plane for too long (if at all) as an overly sentimental ghost is counterproductive.

If ghosts who choose to remain on the astral plane become troublesome to the living, or where there is a service-based requirement to assist them, they may be communicated with on that plane and, if they agree, encouraged to move on and be escorted to the threshold of the mental plane by a living human being who acts as a psychopomp. There is an additional point that needs to be considered in this section, which is the risk of destructive jinn possessing ghosts on the astral plane, delaying their progress, and then using that form to attempt to cause harm to living human beings.

In these cases, exorcism of the possessing jinn is required, followed by an attempt to assist the ghost in making the transition to the mental plane. I have provided an example of this phenomenon, albeit mistakenly identified in that case, in the previous section on the Shadow People.

SUPERNATURAL OBJECTS

That antique pendant you own may be alive, you know. It may have an energy of its own. A consciousness. A unique purpose. Have you felt uncomfortable in its presence? Strangely attracted to it? Or ambivalent? Has it brought warmth into your home or incited nightmares?

The notion of beings such as jinn possessing objects is not unfamiliar to most people, from Aladdin's lamp to "Chucky," and even though it may sound incredible and far removed from reality, the phenomenon is extremely common. For that reason, it is important to have a working knowledge of this area of the paranormal to head off unwanted interferences by destructive jinn or harmful thought forms created either consciously or unconsciously by human beings.

The Occult Artwork

A couple of years ago, an occult anthology came into my possession. I was surprised and delighted to find that the book contained a high-quality, loose-leaf glossy print of an abstract occult painting by an apparently well-known artist in the occult community. I removed the print from the book and set it down on my desk. Almost immediately, I began to detect a malevolent presence in the images on the print. At first, I tried to quash my feelings of unease; I liked the print and wanted to display it in my study. The last thing I wanted to do was to get rid of it.

Yet, the feeling of apprehension persisted.As I looked at the abstract image in the ensuing days, I realized that it wasn't as abstract as I had initially thought; I could make out a grotesque being with huge eyes and a protruding skull amid the swirls and lines. I slipped it into its folder to cover the image while I considered my options.

My dawning awareness brought with it an increase of activity on the part of the being, which began to assert itself more aggressively. For instance, on one occasion I was standing on one side of the room examining a book, when I was startled by the print mysteriously sliding out of its cardboard folder, followed almost immediately by an object falling from a cupboard in the room onto my altar, in the absence of any breeze in the room. The being clearly wanted to get my attention.

Tarot divination showed me that the entity was harmful and that it was attempting to obsess me and draw me toward it. Turning to my spirit guides for assistance, I was told in no uncertain terms to ceremonially burn the print and to get rid of the ashes in a particular manner. I promptly carried out those instructions, albeit with a sense of regret at the destruction of a work of art that I had admired. The energetic disturbances and feelings of foreboding disappeared immediately.

Reflecting on that experience, my strong instinct (backed up by divination) was that someone—most likely the artist—had deliberately co-opted a jinn to work through the medium of art, perhaps to make the impact of the art more potent, but unwittingly giving the jinn free rein to cause harm.

The theme of deception is common when it comes to the jinn, which is a very compelling reason to exercise caution in interacting with them—they are notorious for lying and manipulating human beings.

The possibility of being misled once caused me much consternation as I navigated my way around a magical quagmire in the form of a mysterious Victorian locket.

The Contacted Locket

I came across the locket online as I was looking for a birthday gift for a friend. The listing described the locket's date of origin as "circa 1890." I would have dismissed it had it not been for the fact that I was immediately struck by the engraving on the locket; it had a specific mystical significance to me, and the timing of my discovery of this symbol appeared to be synchronistic.

Immediately after purchasing the locket, misgivings began to set in. Before the locket had even arrived, I began to detect an unusual energy in connection with it. Even remotely, it had a powerful and intimidating presence, and I sensed a malevolent energy around it.

Tarot divination suggested that I consult my spirit guides and that the locket was indeed connected to an undesirable entity—and also to some kind of elemental being. It seemed important that something was magically bound or contained. Yet, despite these ominous signs, the overall message seemed to be that the locket was meant to be mine.

It occurred to me that the seller—a vintage and antiques dealer—might be in a position to shed some light on the locket's past. His response provided no illumination.

It's an unusual piece; I have owned it for some years; sorry but I have no history for it.

I wondered what he meant by "unusual."

A few days later the locket arrived. I knew immediately that I must not open it. Opening it would imply acceptance and that I would effectively be giving permission to any harmful beings to latch on to me, since the potential for an energetic link between the locket and me had been established as soon as I had become conscious of its energy.

I wrapped the entire package in a piece of fabric and stowed it away in a consecrated garment. My overriding instinct was to wait for further instructions. I had to trust that the answers would come to me. Nevertheless, I felt uneasy. Patience is not my strong point, and I was distinctly uncomfortable at the prospect of a destructive presence apparently at large in my home as I grappled with seemingly elusive answers.

Days later, I consciously sought out help from my spirit guides, who told me that the locket had "chosen" me and that I must exercise extreme caution when handling it. They said that it contained an extremely volatile deity, that I must not remove it from its packaging until further notice, and that I would need to work with the locket in time. Also, they said, a jinn was attached to it.

Time passed, and I began to feel increasingly uncomfortable in the room where I had stowed the locket. I performed an exorcism using my ritual sword,[1] and the presence disappeared.

More time passed, and I reflected further on the situation. Out of the blue, I recalled a dream that I'd had a month before purchasing the locket. In the dream, I had been performing a powerful exorcism using my ritual sword. Afterward, I had been told in vision that "a great danger" was coming to me and that I "must not accept gifts from strangers." If I were to accept a gift, I would have to deal with a great "evil." This seemed to explain why I had instinctively refused to "accept" the locket by opening the package. It was strange that the dream had remained dormant in my consciousness for so long.

Eventually, I received the answers that I needed. It seemed that the locket had been contacted by a magician a long time ago. By "contacted," I mean the magician had energetically linked the locket to a powerful elemental being. He had misused the being's power through the locket for selfish ends. My sense was that he was merely one piece in the jigsaw puzzle. Nonetheless, the collateral damage caused by this individual's abuse of the being would become evident to me in the coming days.

I was given instructions to unwrap the locket on a specific date and to immediately cleanse it with holy water so as to clear away the residual negative energy from its past. It was free of harmful influences, they said, but I had work to do and must wear the locket for limited periods of time for that purpose. No one else was to touch the locket, since the being was dangerous, and under no circumstances was I to render myself subservient to the being by worshiping it.

I duly followed those instructions, cleansing the locket with holy water and asserting my authority over the being shortly before I went to bed on the prescribed date. I wore the locket from time to time as I was instructed to by the higher beings who were working with me.

I was awoken in the early hours of the following morning after two disturbing dreams. In the first dream, a lineage of women—all standing together at the same time—struggled to rein in destructive forces. I saw a way through the difficulties.

In the second, more visceral, dream, I saw pools of blood in a forest and heard a woman's screams as she was being pursued. As I awoke, I had a vision of a flag that was completely unfamiliar to me, and reference was made to "Pinochet." Research revealed that the flag had a very specific South American navy commander connection. In that context, "Pinochet" appeared to relate to Augusto Pinochet, the Chilean dictator who was responsible for overthrowing the Chilean government and was behind the gratuitous deaths of thousands of people after a military coup in 1973.

It is not evident to me precisely how the locket fits into the events in South America during Pinochet's command, or indeed who had owned it at the time, but it seems to have been materially involved through its contacted elemental in the assertion of force to control others—apparently women in particular.

My dreams were showing me a part of the locket's history and its potential for significant harm. Somehow, I had been involved in the breaking of a destructive cycle on the astral plane that had persisted long after the drama had played out on the physical plane. I didn't need to know the details of my involvement; I just needed to ensure that I was tuned into my higher guidance to ensure that my actions were aligned with the will of the Divine.

The Tibetan Tapestries

My husband I once went on a yoga retreat in the south of Spain.

On arrival at the retreat center, which is very popular in the global yoga community, we were immediately struck by the vast numbers of statues of religious deities scattered around the retreat grounds, often in excessive quantities. The deities were from a variety of different Eastern pantheons, and I was acutely conscious that it was never a good idea for devas who were affiliated with disparate religions to be colocated on the same property or in the same room, given the propensity for energetic conflicts between them.

It was the height of summer and extremely hot, but our room was air-conditioned and its windows therefore remained closed. There were two silken Tibetan wall hangings depicting abstract patterns on the wall of the bedroom, overlooking the bed. I immediately disliked them. Curiously, there was a covering on each wall hanging, allowing the viewer either to conceal or reveal the abstract patterns. The coverings had been tied back by default, revealing the patterns.

Toward dusk on the first night, my husband and I returned to our room and, upon opening the door, were immediately confronted with a swarm of flies, the likes of which neither of us had ever seen before. They were in between the fly screen and the window itself, but the window and door had remained closed the entire day. The retreat center staff were as surprised as we were. We had no option but to get rid of the flies by using a noxious insecticide spray, pending an inspection by maintenance staff the next day.

The following day, we left our room again in the morning, returning at various intervals, making sure to seal the room off completely while we were away. We even asked the cleaning staff not to clean the room, to mitigate any risk of the windows being opened, which would have exposed the room to further risk of infestation. A member of the maintenance team inspected the room thoroughly but wasn't able to identify any apertures that would have enabled the flies to enter. He was absolutely mystified. Later that afternoon, I returned to the room, and something told me to open the fly screen. Another swarm of flies flew out from behind the closed fly screen, from the *inside* of the closed window. There was no logical explanation for the reappearance of the flies.

At that point, it occurred to me that paranormal activity was very likely to blame. Swarms of *flies* in particular are a common physical manifestation of jinn or, in mainstream Western terminology, demonic activity. My husband and I separately arrived at the same conclusion: that the flies were linked to the Tibetan wall hangings, the origins of which were unknown to us and no doubt to the retreat center owner, who had clearly picked up an extensive collection of authentic religious artifacts during her world travels.

We covered up the wall hangings and removed them from the wall. The fly infestations immediately stopped and didn't return for the remainder of our stay.

Some things to take away from these experiences are, first, to be mindful of the objects that you encounter outside the home, such as hotels and other people's homes, and, second, to be alert to any nagging feelings that something in your possession is off, however irrational they may appear. Just as objects such as jewelry can be used as magical amulets (or protective devices) or talismans (to achieve specific purposes), they are often used by human beings who are skilled in the occult for harmful purposes, usually by co-opting deva entities. It is also well worth investigating the history of articles that you are of a mind to buy in antique stores, over the internet, and so on.

FIVE

DIVINITY

The Tao is infinite, eternal.
Why is it eternal?
It was never born;
thus it can never die.
Why is it infinite?
It has no desires for itself;
thus it is present for all beings.

The Master stays behind;
that is why she is ahead.
She is detached from all things;
that is why she is one with them.
Because she has let go of herself,
she is perfectly fulfilled.
—Stanza 7, *Tao Te Ching—Lao Tzu*[1]
...

A part from using the term "God" to refer to the ineffable entity that I refer to elsewhere in this book as "Divinity" or—as it was revealed to me—"the Source," human beings also tend to use "god" to describe a variety of lesser beings who sit "beneath" Divinity in the cosmic hierarchy.

It is clearly incorrect to put the Source into the same ideological bucket as those conditional beings that religious texts have variously describe as idols or false gods—terms that have become loaded with religious propaganda.

Even the creator deities who issue from the union of the Source and matter are in the process of evolution to iron out the creases of their imperfection, much like all other beings, including humanity. These powerful yet imperfect gods are tasked with creating the stages on which evolution must play out: the earth, the solar system, the cosmos. The gods who are tasked with creating worlds are imperfect gods of the cosmos, born of the thought of something other than the infinite perfection of the absolute that cannot be relegated to a conditional concept.

I use the term "thought"[2] deliberately. If you cast your mind back to chapter 1, you will recall the importance of the mental plane in the process of creation. Since thinking is inherently creative and therefore imperfect, thought itself is in opposition to Divinity in its absolute sense.

So perfect is the Source that it cannot be involved in the messy business of creation. Instead, the Source must forever observe the process of evolution unfolding in a cosmos in which it is merely reflected.

Helena Blavatsky summarizes this dichotomy very clearly in *The Secret Doctrine:*[3]

The One is infinite and unconditioned. It cannot create, for It can have no relation to the finite and conditioned. If everything we see, from the glorious suns and planets down to the blades of grass and the specks of dust, had been created by the Absolute Perfection and were the direct work of even the First Energy that proceeded from It, then every such thing would have been perfect, eternal, and unconditioned, like its author. The millions upon millions of imperfect works found in Nature testify loudly that they are the products of finite, conditioned beings—though the latter were and are Dhyân Chohans, Archangels, or whatever else they may be named. In short, these imperfect works are the unfinished production of evolution, under the guidance of the imperfect Gods.

...

In some respects, Blavatsky's views on cosmogony aren't too far away from modern scientific thinking: I recently watched a TikTok video of a thirteen-year-old physics genius (perhaps an unwitting sage) explaining that in their view, the Source is pure energy.

Despite our apparent separation from Divinity, as I explain in chapter 1, human beings are inexorably linked to Spirit through the higher aspects of the mental body. Perfection of the soul through countless incarnations into human form means that we are of a suitable substance so as to be able to reunite with Divinity as spirit until we recommence the process of reincarnation at the birth of a new cosmic age, manifesting in more elevated forms.

One might be forgiven for concluding, ironically, that the evolutionary scheme is fundamentally nihilistic. We humans are reduced to glorified cogs in a wheel in a much larger wheel to give effect to an impersonal process as we are deliberately made to struggle through life.

Yet, it may be helpful to consider how far we have already traveled and what creative inspiration might be available to us should we persevere. Our suffering as human beings is perhaps unique; the state of our consciousness, our ability to think effectively, makes us infinitely more sensitive (and potentially crueler) than even the most evolved members of the animal kingdom. Yet, we have not fully mastered a consciousness conducive to letting go of our anguish. There is a mystical significance to humanity's positioning in the cosmos—the learning curve is a singularly steep one.

SIX

EVIL

Do you want to improve the world?
I don't think it can be done.

The world is sacred.
It can't be improved.
If you tamper with it, you'll ruin it.
If you treat it like an object, you'll lose it.

There is a time for being ahead,
a time for being behind;
a time for being in motion,
a time for being at rest;
a time for being vigorous,
a time for being exhausted;
a time for being safe,
a time for being in danger.

The Master sees things as they are,
without trying to control them.
She lets them go their own way,
and resides at the center of the circle.
—Stanza 29, *Tao Te Ching*—Lao Tzu[1]
...

A crucial part of the evolutionary challenge for humanity is learning how to deal with opposition, including those dichotomous aspects of selfhood—the light and the "shadow." Since the imperfect universe fundamentally operates in pairs of opposites or polarities, we must expect the process of destruction to follow creation. Likewise, where there is a desire to evolve, there must be a desire to halt that evolution in its tracks. The two opposing forces that we tend to generalize as "good" and "evil" must work themselves out through friction before finally coming into balance.

We tell this primeval story in our fairy tales; it fascinates and entertains us on Netflix. But how much attention do we pay to the deeper messages? To what extent do we distort those messages? Good usually prevails over evil; yet, in reality, a balance must be struck between the two. It is misleading to suggest that "good" and "evil" are anything other than relative concepts, since they are two different sides of the same coin, the reconciling whole of which is greater than the sum of its parts.

There is no evil counterpart to the Source, since the Source is perfect. For that reason, I have deliberately not dealt with "Divinity" and "Evil" in the same chapter.

If we step a level down from the Source, into a universe of duality (and, therefore, imperfection), we need to take into account the fact that the various planets and planetoids in our solar system are similarly experiencing divergent states of evolution, giving rise to the notion of cosmic "evil" insofar as the differences in evolution give rise to conflict. It is for that reason that Alice A. Bailey makes a distinction between "sacred" and "non-sacred" planets. She classifies Earth as one of the "non-sacred" planets since Earth has not yet fully evolved.[2]

Allow me to take this explanation a little further.

As I mention in chapter 1, humanity as it is currently incarnating on Earth is operating under the influence of the Law of Attraction, which concerns Spirit, and means that human beings have the capacity to reach a point of evolution that enables them to work consciously with Spirit (or cocreate) through the soul to create the forms *that are needed by the soul.*

On the other hand, some other planets and planetary beings are entrenched in a less advanced, more separative state of evolution, which is focused solely on matter, the development of the personality, and the following of the path of least resistance.[3] These beings do not have the capacity to consciously respond to the evolutionary calling available to human beings. This is a very important point to bear in mind in dealing with other beings.

Earth is therefore in conflict with planets populated by beings who are less evolved than human beings. That doesn't mean that beings who are in conflict with humanity are necessarily less technologically evolved—on the contrary, they seem to have many skills and technologies that surpass those of humanity. Equally, far be it from humanity to purport to impose value judgments on these beings when human beings as a species continue to grapple with the good-evil polarity (i.e., we are far from perfect ourselves), and we have come a long way on our own evolutionary journey.

The planetary gods associated with different planets are evolving according to the same principles that govern humanity's evolution. They are therefore the embodiment at a macrocosmic level of the state of evolution of the planet that they govern. The separate nature of certain planets and planetoids means that planetary gods will be opposed to each other, and the beings who populate them will be fundamentally at odds with humanity. This means that they are fundamentally opposed to human goals and consciously will humanity's setback and destruction.

At some point in a conflict between two planets, a third planetary god that embodies a higher state of evolution will intervene, permitting the reconciliation of spirit and matter, thereby eradicating the cosmic evil.[4] This process will eventually occur at some point in the case of conflicts between Earth and other planets. Until then, human beings must continue to struggle with opposing forces. As I discuss in chapter 7, it is likely that the asteroid Hygiea is already active in the capacity of mediator between Earth and other less evolved planets.

In addition, it is important to bear in mind that in humanity's distant past, human beings were far less evolved from the point of view of soul; they incarnated in a state that was completely separate from Spirit and were therefore under the influence of fundamentally separative or destructive deities who were connected to the physical planes of humanity *at that point in humanity's evolution*. These beings are, unfortunately, still in existence and continue to influence humanity today. They are connected to even more powerful deities who are the embodiment of a lesser state of evolution and, therefore, cosmic evil.

This is problematic for two reasons: first, these beings can and do influence human beings, such as individuals who practice "black magic" and individuals who have an affinity to these deities (such as through working with them in previous incarnations). This means that even those members of human society who appear to have no interest in the occult, including extremely powerful and influential members of society, are susceptible to influence by them. Some of those humans may rise to power over lifetimes as they consciously work with the more powerful entities who represent evil on a cosmic scale, potentially causing significant setbacks to the unfoldment of humanity's current evolution as it is exercised through the Law of Attraction. An example of that type of evil in action is in the use of mass fear as an instrument to manipulate human beings. Second, choosing to work with these destructive beings has severe consequences for the soul. I discuss those consequences in chapter 8.

It is important, therefore, that we cultivate awareness of these destructive beings so that we can deal with them effectively and exercise our judgment soundly when we come into contact with human beings who are not acting for the highest good of humanity. Awareness helps sharpen our intuition and strengthen our inner resilience and self-autonomy in identifying circumstances where we might otherwise be playing into the hands of destructive beings; for example, by buying into and feeding fear culture. Such fear has been rife in the context of the coronavirus pandemic and is energized by the mass media.

In cultivating awareness of these forces and by developing our knowledge of the soul and how it interacts with the myriad of other beings who are intricately involved in our evolution, we can consciously distance ourselves from the destructive elements and work more constructively with those beings such as the solar angels who are working in our interests.

SEVEN

THE CONSCIOUS UNIVERSE

There was something formless and perfect
before the universe was born.
It is serene. Empty.
Solitary. Unchanging.
Infinite. Eternally present.
It is the mother of the universe.
For lack of a better name,
I call it the Tao.

It flows through all things,
inside and outside, and returns
to the origin of all things.

The Tao is great.
The universe is great.
Earth is great.
Man is great.
These are the four great powers.

Man follows the earth.
Earth follows the universe.
The universe follows the Tao.
The Tao follows only itself.
—Stanza 25, *Tao Te Ching*—*Lao Tzu*[1]
...

A s I outlined in chapter 1, human beings are etherically tuned into the etheric body of humanity as a whole, which is in turn part of the etheric body of Earth and other planets in the solar system.

Our solar system is likewise connected to the etheric bodies of six other solar systems, and through them to seven higher energy centers, forming a vast network for the distribution of certain "conditioning" (or influencing) energies or rays.

The hermetic axiom "As above, so below" (or the principle that the microcosm reflects the macrocosm) means that the dynamics that play out in the cosmos are precisely replicated on a microscopic scale on Earth, and so human beings not only embody the form and energies of higher beings on a lesser scale but are directly affected by cosmic patterning.

As part of that overarching framework, certain transformative streams of energy flow through to Earth from three particular star systems: Ursa Major ("the Great Bear"), the Pleiades, and Sirius[2] —in a similar way that the sun's radiation affects the earth. The seven solar systems are astrologically connected to these constellations, but human beings become "occultly" tuned into the effects of these constellations only once they are aware of the vibration of Divinity through the soul. In other words, human beings develop the necessary "equipment" to tune into and work with the frequency of those constellations only once they have developed awareness of the soul and are in touch with Divinity.

As the majority of human beings continue to slumber, unaware of the presence of the soul, these ray energies filter through to Earth through the sun via the other planets in our solar system and materially impact humanity through the seven chakras or energy centers in the etheric body of human beings.

This system of energy and rays is the fundamental basis of the practice of astrology, which is, contrary to popular belief, far from a mere psychological construct of the planets (or as the Greeks called them, the "wandering stars"), coincidentally reflecting events on Earth.

The purpose of the streams of energy as they are conditioned by the constellations is fundamentally one of transmutation. The purpose of this transmutation is to give effect to the will of Divinity: operating in certain triangular configurations, such as trilateral interactions between the planets themselves,[3] they shape the consciousness of the cosmos (including humanity and the other beings that I refer to in chapter 4), taking it from a lower state to a higher state of being. In other words, these streams of energy underpin the entire process of evolution.

It is natural to feel a level of discomfort at the thought that ultimately, we human beings have very limited control over the will of Divinity; yet, it is futile to buck against a system that is so massively beyond our "pay grades" within the cosmos. We didn't create the universe—we are simply intelligent cogs in the wheels of that gargantuan ecosystem, with some scope to make intelligent decisions and to evolve and eventually make our way back to the Source.

Alice A. Bailey refers to the seven planets that transmit rays directly to the seven chakras as "sacred planets."[4] Some of them are not officially recognized as true planets by modern astronomy (or even among most modern astrologers), which isn't surprising, since their effect is profoundly esoteric. They are:

- Vulcan

- Mercury

- Venus

- Jupiter

- Saturn

- Neptune

- Uranus

There are also five "non-sacred" planets,[5] which, though unconnected to the chakra centers, do emit radiation to humanity (and, in the case of the sun, synthesize energy). They are:

- the sun

- the moon

- Earth

- Mars

- Pluto

Together, these twelve planets (as they govern the astrological houses or places of significance in an astrological chart) condition the human personality and relate to the external life and circumstances of human beings. In effect, the planets limit the consciousness of human beings until they have done the work necessary to evolve.[6]

By contrast, the twelve constellations of the astrological zodiac condition the human soul; as I mentioned earlier in this chapter, this dynamic becomes active at a point in an individual's evolution when they are operating from the perspective of the soul rather than merely through the personality. At that stage, although the individual continues to feel the influence of the planets very strongly, their impact begins to dwindle until, eventually, they are no longer able to limit an individual's ability to develop their consciousness.

As you may know from conventional or mainstream astrology, the energies of the planets blend with the energies of the twelve constellations, and particular configurations or patterns are identifiable in an individual horoscope or birth chart. These configurations must be read in light of the individual's relative evolution to distinguish personality aspects from soul aspects in a chart.

The differences in astrological interpretation that arise as a result of the relative control of the planets over the person seeking a reading (as dictated by the person's particular state of development) will inevitably give rise to some inaccuracies in readings, which is why it is important that astrologers are selected with care, depending on the purpose of the astrological consultation. For example, it would be inaccurate for an astrologer to suggest that someone with a highly developed consciousness will absolutely fall victim to a challenging planetary configuration in the natal chart at a particular moment in time. This is because the person is likely to have evolved to a point where they are able to respond to the challenge in a constructive and empowering way, exercising right judgment, since they are attuned to the overriding influence of the constellations, and the influence of the planets over them is far weaker.

Streams of energy are, therefore, transmitted to humanity via Earth both cosmically through the planets and systemically through the constellations. This energetic duality is pivotal to humanity and informs the wider theme of duality that pervades the development of every human being.[7] This duality derives from one of the seven major rays that transmit energy to humanity: the second ray (or the ray of "love-wisdom"). This ray concerns itself with humanity's current evolutionary goal, which is governed by a system that Alice refers to as the "second aspect," which I discuss in more detail in chapter 8: the ability to cocreate with Spirit.

"Love-wisdom" is an elevated form of desire for something outside oneself. When we are engaging in "love-wisdom," we are consciously building a form for something that is consistent with what the *soul* needs, rather than to feed the personality. This concept is integral to the Law of Attraction since our ability to manifest is impeded when we are not in alignment with who we really are. When we are out of alignment, we may unconsciously manifest things that are detrimental to us—or we simply won't manifest anything at all.

This points right back to the importance of developing inner reflection tools such as meditation to ensure that you are in tune with your soul and understand what it is calling for, free of interference from the limited personality. There is no silver-bullet solution that will magically switch on this intuition; it requires ongoing development and the expression of conscious intention to be in touch with the higher mind. If you seek guidance from others on what your soul needs, beware of frauds and advice from so-called experts who have not yet done the necessary soul work themselves and are therefore not "qualified" to give you pure advice for the highest good, free from the biases of their personalities.

While we cannot escape our interconnectivity with the cosmos and its governing system under the unifying principle of the Law of Attraction, it is important that we honor our individuality, making wise choices on our individual journeys rather than following the path of least resistance, which is a feature of the world of form, the "third aspect" (with its goal of "active intelligence") that humanity is no longer aspiring toward, which I discuss in more detail in chapter 8. We unlocked the aspirations of "active intelligence" a long time ago, and it is now time to move forward and to embrace "love-wisdom" or prudent manifestation.

The chakras in the human body correspond to the seven sacred planets and determine the particular streams of consciousness or "rays" on which the efforts of individual human beings are principally focused in the lifetime, according to their evolutionary progress. The activity of the chakras galvanizes a person's "ray tendency."[8] When a person is operating exclusively from the perspective of the personality, they are influenced by the chakras below the diaphragm (at the base of the spine, the sacrum, and the solar plexus), as well as by the energetic center at the spleen. The constellations of the zodiac are active, but the planets are determinative of the unfoldment of consciousness. This means that the individual has less control over their destiny.

Focusing on the development of personality is another aspect of the aspiration of the systemic "third aspect"; it is no longer relevant to humanity since we now have the capacity to develop soul consciousness. While many human beings remain unaware of their capacity for soul growth, the critical difference is that in the current human epoch or great cycle, we have the potential to develop such awareness if not in the current lifetime, in future lifetimes, whereas in the previous epoch, which was dominated by matter, we simply didn't have the inner "technology" to develop the soul.

Where a person is operating from the perspective of soul rather than personality, the chakras above the diaphragm (at the heart, throat, third eye, and crown) are activated, and the person comes under the influence of Ursa Major, the Pleiades, and Sirius (as well as the zodiacal constellations), but the grip of the planets on the personality is loosened, meaning that the person has more scope to change the outcome of their destiny as it appears in the birth chart.

The subject of the transformative effect of the rays through the constellations is immense, and a far more comprehensive and granular discussion, including a complete analysis of the individual rays, may be found in Alice A. Bailey's *Esoteric Astrology*;[9] however, the basic principles are an important part of the equipment that we need to inform our understanding of the place of human beings in the cosmos and the dynamics that give rise to our evolution.

As Alice briefly observes in *A Treatise on Cosmic Fire*,[10] asteroids exert a material influence over the planets, which warrants future research, particularly in the context of cosmic "evil."

The asteroid Hygiea is potentially a rich avenue for further study. Significant progress has been made in the field of sound healing in the Acutonics system of integrated medicine in relation to the frequency associated with Hygiea. Hygiea operates multidimensionally to cleanse and purify, bringing together the various disparate pieces of an entity to form a whole, reconciling polarities. She is very much associated with the notion of a planetary upgrade and the integration of spirit and matter. It seems very likely that Hygiea is already instrumentally involved (as a third or mediatory "planet") in the reconciliation of the conflict between Earth and other less evolved planets. To that end, I work with the Hygiea sound frequency in administering sound healing where there is a need to integrate both spirit and matter to achieve a more elevated potential.

EIGHT

JUDICIOUS AWAKENING

*And the soul of the true philosopher thinks that she ought not to resist this deliverance,
and therefore abstains from pleasures and desires and pains and fears, as far as she
is able; reflecting that when a man has great joys or sorrows or fears or desires, he
suffers from them, not merely the sort of evil which might be anticipated—as for
example, the loss of his health or property which he has sacrificed to his lusts—but
an evil greater far, which is the greatest and worst of all evils, and one of which he
never thinks.*
"What is it, Socrates?" said Cebes.
*The evil is that when the feeling of pleasure or pain is most intense, every soul of
man imagines the objects of this intense feeling to be then plainest and truest: but
this is not so, they are really the things of sight.*
Very true.
And is not this the state in which the soul is most enthralled by the body?
How so?
*Why, because each pleasure and pain is a sort of nail which nails and rivets the
soul to the body, until she becomes like the body, and believes that to be true which
the body affirms to be true; and from agreeing with the body and having the same
delights she is obliged to have the same habits and haunts, and is not likely ever to
be pure at her departure to the world below, but is always infected by the body; and
so she sinks into another body and there germinates and grows, and has therefore
no part in the communion of the divine and pure and simple.*
Most true, Socrates, answered Cebes.
*And this, Cebes, is the reason why the true lovers of knowledge are temperate and
brave; and not for the reason which the world gives.*
Certainly not.
　　　—"Phaedo," in Plato: Complete Works, translated by Benjamin Jowlett[1]

...

In *A Treatise on Cosmic Fire*,[2] Alice A. Bailey distinguishes between three different functioning paradigms that operate in relation to all living things below the level of Divinity; she refers to these states as the third, second, and first "aspects," respectively relating to matter (governed by the Law of Economy), spirit (governed by the Law of Attraction), and the reconciliation of the two opposites of matter and spirit (governed by the Law of Synthesis).[3] All beings encompass these three aspects, but some are dominated by one or another of them. An example is those beings who are associated with planets dominated by the third aspect (or matter), which I discuss earlier in this book.

As I mentioned in chapter 7, having moved beyond a dominant third aspect, leaning toward following the separative path of least resistance, with its focus on personality rather than the development of consciousness, humanity is currently able to effectively leverage the systemic second aspect. We can do this by developing our consciousness and the ability to cocreate with Spirit by creating specific forms in alignment with the intelligent desire of the soul, through a mixture of astral and mental substances (the combination of desire and mind).[4]

At some point, humanity will aspire as a group to the concept of synthesis or union inherent in the first aspect (we experience this as individuals when we evolve to a point where we are able to achieve union with self, thereby escaping to Spirit, eventually merging with the Source).

Against the backdrop of what is currently possible for humanity from an evolutionary perspective, the starting point of the process for the individual human being is becoming awakened to and aware of higher truths, including the existence of the enduring soul, through the intervention of spirit guides and the higher mind with its link to Divinity. This awakening is *not* about being "woke." It's about genuine, balanced spiritual growth, which involves consciously examining the shadows or dualities within oneself and doing the work necessary to reconcile the conflicting polarities by tuning into Spirit—just like the process that is currently underway at a macrocosmic level between the planetary deities in the cosmos.

A crucial part of that process is understanding how to avoid falling into obvious traps, such as doing things without fully researching the consequences or with the aim of feeding the demands of the personality, with its associated insecurities and hubris. There is also an element of having to effectively manage change in the context of the unfolding awareness as one navigates the spiritual path in a mundane (albeit slowly awakening) world.

THE RISKS OF PREMATURE RAISING
OF ENERGY

In chapter 1, I discussed fire by friction or kundalini fire and its function of animating and vitalizing the physical body.

The notion of kundalini as an active or emanating fire associated with the physical body is one with which many of you will be familiar; it tends to be bandied about liberally in spiritual settings (ironically, even in the context of the practice of kundalini yoga itself), in the absence of any granular discussion of precisely what it is and what it does—and what the associated risks are.

Unfortunately, there is generally an assumption that kundalini should be consciously raised from the base of the spine to bring about spiritual awakening. The unsettling symptoms that often ensue as a result of this process, such as convulsing, crying, hysterical laughter, and antisocial behaviors, are either recklessly disregarded or incorrectly dismissed as natural side effects that are to be expected. I suspect that I witnessed this firsthand as a participant in a pranayama class, when advanced breathing techniques provoked hysterical sobbing from another participant.

It is dangerous to engage the Sushumna (one of the three etheric channels housed in the spinal column) before an effective link between Divinity and the personality has been established. In the absence of such a link, the kundalini energy will rise unmitigated by the downward flow of Spirit, burning away the protective etheric barrier before the individual is ready to come into direct contact with the astral plane.

The Sushumna plays a significant role in the rising of kundalini; that process will safely occur only once the Ida and Pingala pathways are working together harmoniously and an appropriate link has been established between the personality and Divinity (independently of the soul) through the building of the so-called rainbow bridge or antahkarana.[5]

The antahkarana connects the crown (or sahasrara) chakra to the personality (that is, the etheric and astral bodies, together with the lower mind). The third eye (or ajna) chakra (located between the eyebrows) becomes active only once construction of the antahkarana has begun; however, the building of this bridge is only really possible when a person begins to operate from the throat (or vishuddha) chakra, expressing themselves authentically and creatively and opening themselves up to higher wisdom in the form of communication from the soul and higher beings.

When prana begins to blend with the kundalini fire at the base of the spine, the kundalini will gradually ascend the spinal column as the vibration of the physical body accelerates and begins to resonate with the higher vibration of the soul.[6] As the kundalini rises, it transfers heat from the energy centers below the solar plexus beneath the breastbone, igniting the three higher chakra centers: the heart, throat, and crown.

The activation of the three higher energy centers causes a change in their action from faintly spinning wheels to four-dimensional wheels of fire, circulating the kundalini and pranic fires. At the same time, the fires of mind (or solar fire) begin to burn with increasing intensity, until they eventually burn away the part of the etheric body (the etheric web) that forms a protective barrier to the crown chakra at the top of the head. Once the etheric web has been removed, Divine wisdom or Spirit can flow downward through the crown chakra, meeting and blending with the upward-flowing kundalini.

Over time, the spinning action of the higher energetic centers brings about a purification of the three spinal column channels and the etheric body, and there is, eventually, nothing to block the spinning of these wheels of kundalini and pranic fire.[7] This is why the sages and adepts of the past (including more modern teachers) have always placed so much emphasis on the process of purification as a means to acquiring spiritual wisdom—cleanliness is close to godliness and so on.

Where a person's thoughts have become purified as they have accessed higher wisdom, so they are able to cleanse their higher chakras, leading eventually to enlightenment. Physical cleanliness is equally important, since on every level the world of form must be conquered before higher aspirations are possible—ongoing physical uncleanliness is usually a strong indication that not all is right in an adult person's life.

When the etheric web disintegrates, the person's etheric body merges with their astral body, giving rise to a continuity of consciousness. So-called astral travel must be understood against this point of technicality—the person may be able to consciously control the movements of their astral body.

I recounted my own experience of the burning away of this etheric web in the preface, when I described my participation in a tai chi retreat in Italy as a young adult. Together with other participants in the class, I had been meditating and consciously moving chi around my body when, in a seated position and with my eyes closed, I experienced the visceral sensation of something pulling at the top of my head and "spilling" over the top of my forehead toward my nose. Although I was familiar with the chakra system at the time, I had no intention of working with my subtle energy centers; nor did I have any intention to deliberately raise my energy to bring about a spiritual awakening.

I am now able to activate my crown chakra at will—and feel that activation through physical sensation. However, bear in mind that my experiences are based on my particular polarization as a soul, according to the energetic rays that govern my current incarnation. My awakening was timed according to a number of variables, including my net karma in this lifetime.

The awakening of the higher centers takes place gradually, according to the polarization of the individual's soul according to the experience that they have acquired over multiple lifetimes and their net karma. This polarization is embodied in the concept of the "rays," which I deal with in chapter 7.

As I have explained above, it is dangerous to raise kundalini in an uncontrolled manner without a simultaneous influx of Divine wisdom to temper the effects of the fire by friction. This tempering process will take the polarization of the individual's soul into account and will help them evolve at a steady yet appropriate pace.

Bearing in mind that the purpose of the etheric vehicle is to protect the individual from premature exposure to astral forces, if the fires are allowed to burn in an uncontrolled manner, they will destroy the etheric vehicle, exposing the individual to serious harm. Alice summarizes this harm as follows:[8]

It will be apparent from this elucidation that the exceeding importance of the etheric vehicles as the separator of the fires has been brought forward, and consequently we have brought to our notice the dangers that must ensue should man tamper injudiciously, ignorantly or willfully with these fires.

Should a man, by the power of will or through an over-development of the mental side of his character, acquire the power to blend these fires of matter and to drive them forward, he stands in danger of obsession, insanity, physical death, or of dire disease in some part of his body, and he also runs the risk of an over-development of the sex impulse through the driving of the force in an uneven manner upwards, or in forcing its radiation to undesirable centers. The reason of this is that the matter of his body is not pure enough to stand the uniting of the flames, that the channel up the spine is still clogged and blocked, and therefore acts as a barrier, turning the flame backwards and downwards, and that the flame (being united by the power of mind and not being accompanied by a simultaneous downflow from the plane of spirit), permits the entrance, through the burning etheric, of undesirable and extraneous forces, currents, and even entities. These wreck and tear and ruin what is left of the etheric vehicle, of the brain tissue and even of the dense physical body itself.

...

It is for those reasons that I would strongly caution against participating in ayahuasca ceremonies and taking other psychedelics in ignorance of the possible risks, before the subtle body is ready for them. In a similar vein, it is important that yoga teachers and other spiritual leaders who teach their students how to actively circulate prana or chi are mindful of the risks, and scrupulous about which students they choose to teach more powerful techniques to.

In the case of beginners, efforts should be focused on the throat chakra to activate the person's higher guidance and to stimulate the building of the rainbow bridge as it connects to the crown chakra, permitting the influx of Divine wisdom, and eventually leading to the activation of the third-eye chakra. At the point that a person is able to access through their inner sight (or senses) the plane above the physical planes of humanity (the fourth ether or buddhic or intuitional plane), they are ready for the burning away of the etheric web from the crown.[9]

The risk of overdeveloping one's mental faculties at the expense of the tempering inflow of higher wisdom (or of not being fully receptive to that wisdom, perhaps as a result of impaired judgment) means that energy work should be avoided if mental illness is present (and is not being effectively managed).

If a person continues to engage in the uncontrolled blending of the fires over multiple lifetimes, they risk severing, through the destruction of their physical permanent atom (which is located in the etheric body), their connection to the soul for the remainder of the period of the solar system, becoming "lost souls." This is because efforts to remove the etheric web by blending the fires in an uncontrolled manner are focused exclusively on the form or matter (and, therefore, from a third aspect or separative perspective) rather than in cooperation with Spirit, which has its aim the evolution of humanity as a whole. Alice says:[10]

> The blending of these fires must be the result of spiritualised knowledge, and must be directed solely by the Light of the Spirit, who works through love and is love, and who seeks this unification and this utter merging not from the point of view of sense or of material gratification, but because liberation and purification is desired in order that the higher union with the Logos may be effected; this union must be desired, not for selfish ends, but because group perfection is the goal and scope for greater service to the race must be achieved.
>
> ...

If you are concerned about reincarnating in a subsequent lifetime in a situation in which you somehow manage to blend the fires in an uncontrolled manner, exposing yourself to the associated risks, the key is to take in this knowledge now and consciously decide to maintain awareness of the risks in subsequent lifetimes. Becoming conscious of matters in the current lifetime is an effective method for assimilating—or banking—the knowledge for the benefit of your future incarnations.

WHY PRACTICING "BLACK" MAGIC IS OBJECTIVELY A BAD IDEA

Just as raising kundalini energy without the cooperation of the Divine is counterintuitive to the evolutionary objectives of humanity as a group (it's basically backward) and, if unchecked through multiple lifetimes, can lead to systemic exile of a partially developed soul for eons upon eons until the next solar system has commenced, so too is the practice of "black" magic (taking the so-called left-hand path) extremely unwise.

Very briefly, the practice of "magic" entails harnessing energies or working with other beings to bring about specified changes or results.

Practicing "black" magic, which is purely selfish in its intent and devoid of the influx of Divine wisdom (or love-wisdom), amounts to an overidentification with the form aspect of the body or the devas who work with form (or both), and therefore an identification with a paradigm of evolution (that is, the third aspect) that humanity has long surpassed. The practitioner is also capable of building an antahkarana (or rainbow bridge) to access their higher faculties, but in this case the practitioner deliberately connects their mental body to certain devas on the mental planes, rather than linking to Spirit through the crown chakra:[11]

Through this medium, and through identification with the devas, he can escape from the three worlds to spheres of evil incomprehensible to us. The point to be remembered here is that the black magician remains ever a prisoner; he cannot escape from substance and from form.

...

As discussed in chapter 6, a very long time ago, human beings were far less evolved from the point of view of soul or consciousness, and, unlike humanity today, which is aspiring to "love-wisdom," they incarnated into a paradigm in which they were working toward the "active intelligence" aim of the third aspect. These human beings were therefore under the influence of certain separative deities who were connected to the physical planes of humanity at that point in humanity's evolution. These beings are still in existence and continue to influence humanity today. They are connected to even more powerful deities who are the embodiment of a lesser state of evolution and, therefore, to cosmic "evil." In that regard, Alice writes:[12]

Black magicians work under certain great Entities, six in number, who are spoken of, for instance, in the Christian Bible as having the number 666. They came in (being cosmic, not systemic) on that stream of force emanating from cosmic mental levels which produced the three worlds of human endeavour. . . . These entities are the sum total of the substance of the three lower subplanes of the cosmic physical plane (our three lower systemic planes), and it is under them that the black magicians are swept into activity, often unconsciously, but rising to power as they work consciously.

...

Alice describes the methodology that a "black magician" follows as a "hindering" of their "evolutionary plan":[13]

> *They center the attention upon the form, and seek to shatter and break that form, or the combination of atoms, in order to permit the central electric life to escape. They bring about this result through external agencies and by availing themselves of the destructive nature of the substance (deva essence) itself. They burn and destroy the material sheath, seeking to imprison the escaping volatile essence as the form disintegrates. This hinders the evolutionary plan in the case of the life involved, delays the consummation, interferes with the ordered progress of development, and puts all the factors involved in a bad position. The life (or entity) concerned receives a setback, the devas work destructively, and without participation in the purpose of the plan, and the magician is in danger, under the Law of Karma, and through the materialising of his own substance by affinity with the third aspect.*
>
> ...

The "black" magician is able to develop their powers in this way since they have access to one-third of the ego's occult capabilities. In addition, the permanent atom relating to matter is active, providing a path to the entities who govern matter where there is intention to reach out to them.[14]

The inherent danger of "black" magic lies in the fact that the human beings who surrender to the artificial and ephemeral promise of power and willfully refuse to progress to the influence of the second aspect, with its "love-wisdom" objective, become "lost souls"; the soul or ego is eventually severed from the personality, and they are exiled from the system until a new solar system is created, at which point they must incarnate into a cycle of "unlimited evil," the experience of which is dictated by the extent of the damage to the severed "egoic body and its innate persistence."[15]

In some cases, human beings simply fail to make the transition to the second aspect; in those cases, they are also exiled from incarnation pending the creation of a new solar system, but the new cycle into which they incarnate is not one of "unlimited evil" or separation.[16]

There is an interesting reference in a footnote to *A Treatise on Cosmic Fire*[17] to an extract from *Mahatma Letters to A. A. Sinnett*, in which the mahatma divides various beings into different categories, one of which is this:

> *Souls or Astral Forms of sorcerers: men who have reached the apex of knowledge in the forbidden art. Dead or alive they have, so to say, cheated nature; but it is only temporary—until our planet goes into obscuration, after which they have nolens volens to be annihilated.*
>
> ...

This suggests that the souls of magicians who have continued to practice black magician to the point of maximum proficiency do not get a second chance at the dawn of a new solar system—they are involuntarily "annihilated."

It is worth pondering on this before yielding to the allure of black magic simply because it contributes to a heady feeling of power and magnetism—and perhaps because it offers a means of projecting very real human feelings of inadequacy, failure, anger, and the like onto other people, ostensibly putting the magician in the driver's seat. It is, of course, a misconception to assume that there is no accountability for that type of magical work. The consequences may last for eternity.

The trouble is that no one ever talks about these consequences in a way that is meaningful to a person who is at a crossroads in their spiritual life; instead, black magic is heavily marketed in the spiritual mainstream. To many, it seems far sexier to be a little rebellious and collaborate with the "dark side," and so black magic attracts a huge following. This provides insight into the likely future of a significant chunk of human beings at the end of the current solar system.

SPIRITUALITY IN A MUNDANE WORLD

Another consequence of the process of genuine awakening is an inevitable diversion from the orthodox, personality-focused path that is followed by the masses, and an accompanying sense of isolation as friends, lovers, and even family may no longer resonate with who you really are. Although there will be others in a similar position to you, these people are likely to be few and far between, and there may be a noticeable dichotomy between the professional life and the personal life.

There are increasing numbers of professional people who are on a spiritual path, particularly after the coronavirus, which sparked a noticeable interest in metaphysical matters as people grappled with certain existential challenges. An awakening consciousness doesn't necessarily require you to terminate your relationship with the corporate world if you are using your skills in a productive way that ultimately serves your path and is part of your "dharma." It may also be necessary for you to operate within that system in a way that serves the greater good. The world needs more influential professionals who are operating in service to the Divine—not for self-aggrandizement but in the interests of the evolution of humanity.

As you discover who you really are and where you are destined to go, on the basis of an increasing awareness of your soul and your connection with the Source, there will, however, come a time where you need to become more discerning about what you communicate to other people, most of whom will be in a very different place from you from the point of view of the development of consciousness; in many cases, other people will be focused purely on personality rather than on conscious cocreation with Spirit.

It is a fool's errand (and inappropriate) to assume that you are doing other, less "enlightened" people a favor by purporting to teach them what you know or by waxing lyrical about a particular spiritual experience—unless they specifically ask you for information. In some cases, the curious may ask you for information, but they are not ready to ingest that information or are simply attempting to goad you—you will therefore need to develop the appropriate judgment to decide when to err on the side of "less is more."

Bearing in mind that we are all etherically connected, the best that you can do in many cases is to focus on raising your own consciousness, and in doing that over time you will begin to raise the consciousness of the people around you.

Since the material in this book is very much on the fringe of society, it may also be worth maintaining a strategic silence to avoid negative judgments and gossip and the resulting negative energy. While some organizations are more open than others and genuinely value diversity of thought, singling yourself out as "different" by sharing unnecessary detail in a way that may not be acceptable to mainstream society is likely to be career limiting. More conservative organizations view staff who stand out in any sort of unconventional way with deep suspicion, despite purporting to value diversity.

Years ago, I took a dowsing crystal[18] with me to work in my pocket—not because I intended to use it at work, but simply because I happened to have it on my person earlier that day and had forgotten to remove it before leaving my home. Unfortunately, it dropped out of my pocket in the ladies' toilets, in front of a senior member of staff who was the epitome of conservatism and reserve. She picked it up and handed it to me with a quizzical expression on her face, and I noticed a distinct change in manner and reticence from her from then on. It is a very natural human reaction to fear the unknown and to exercise conscious or unconscious bias.

These days, in the paradigm of the "cancel culture," staff handbooks and social media policies are particularly stringent around engaging in any activities that could bring organizations into disrepute. It is therefore worth reviewing these policies carefully and ensuring that you stay on the right side of them should you wish to hold on to your job.

ENDNOTES

INTRODUCTION

1. Alice A. Bailey, *Esoteric Astrology* (London: Lucis, 2017).
2. The Organization for Professional Astrology. The OPA describes itself as "a non-profit organization that advances the cause of professional astrology by helping students and practicing astrologers receive the information, insights, and experiences they need to foster their understanding of astrology, launch a professional practice, or enhance their development."
3. H. P. Blavatsky, *The Secret Doctrine* (Kindle edition: Strelbytskyy Multimedia, 2022), 2944.

1: DECODING THE SOUL

1. Benjamin Jowett, trans., *Laws by Plato*, Kindle edition, 236.
2. There are some exceptions to immortality of the soul—see chapter 6.
3. Jeffrey Henderson, *Plato IX* (Cambridge, MA: Harvard University Press, 1929), 99.
4. "Ego" in this context is intended to refer to the personality, not to the soul (as defined later on in chapter 1).

The human Body and its planes of consciousness

1. Alice A. Bailey, *A Treatise on Cosmic Fire* (London: Lucis, 2017), section 2, 308.
2. Alice A. Bailey, *Esoteric Healing* (London: Lucis, 2016), 490.
3. Bailey, *A Treatise on Cosmic Fire*, 97–98.
4. Bailey, *Esoteric Healing*, 72.
5. Bailey, *Esoteric Astrology*, 10.
6. Ibid., 352.
7. Ibid., 10–11.
8. Ibid., 352.
9. Bailey, *A Treatise on Cosmic Fire*, 47.
10. Ibid., 332.
11. Ibid., section 2, 308.
12. Ibid., 55.
13. Ibid., 544–45.
14. Ibid., 332.
15. Alice A. Bailey, *Esoteric Psychology I* (London: Lucis, 2018), 58–59.

16. Michael Newton, *Journey of Souls Case Studies of Life between Lives* (Woodbury, MN: Llewellyn, 2017).
17. Bailey, *Esoteric Psychology I*, 41.
18. Ibid., 54.
19. Bailey, *A Treatise on Cosmic Fire*, 45–47.
20. See Alice A. Bailey, *A Treatise on Cosmic Fire*, section 1, 37.
21. Bailey, *A Treatise on Cosmic Fire*, 46.

Reincarnation and Karma

1. Benjamin Jowlett, trans., "Phaedo," in *Plato: Complete Works*, Kindle edition, 12099.
2. Bailey, *A Treatise on Cosmic Fire*, 791.
3. Bailey, *A Treatise on Cosmic Fire*, 798.

The Process of Ensoulment

1. Jowlett, "Phaedrus," in *Plato: Complete Works*, Kindle edition, 25410.
2. Newton, *Journey of Souls Case Studies of Life between Lives*.
3. Referred to by Alice A. Bailey as the "devachan" state of consciousness on the mental plane.
4. Newton, *Journey of Souls Case Studies of Life between Lives*, 267.
5. Bailey, *A Treatise on Cosmic Fire*, 505–506.
6. Ibid., 315.
7. Ibid., 944.
8. Ibid., 114.
9. Yogic breathing exercises.

The Law of Attraction

1. Bailey, *A Treatise on Cosmic Fire*, 595, footnote 85.
2. Bailey, *A Treatise on Cosmic Fire*, Kindle edition, 933.

2: DEATH

1. Frances Lincoln, *Tao Te Ching—Lao Tzu* (London: Frances Lincoln, 2013).
2. Jowlett, "Phaedrus," in *Plato: Complete Works*, Kindle edition, 49615.
3. See Alice A. Bailey, *Esoteric Healing*, part 2, 380; and Michael Newton, *Journey of Souls Case Studies of Life between Lives*.
4. Bailey, *Esoteric Healing*, 419.
5. Bailey, *Esoteric Healing*, part 2, 380.

3: DISEASE

1. Lincoln, *Tao Te Ching—Lao Tzu.*
2. Bailey, *Esoteric Healing,* part 1, 9.
3. Bailey, *Esoteric Healing,* 69–70.
4. Ibid., 80.
5. Ibid., 79.

4: OTHER BEINGS

1. Lincoln, *Tao Te Ching—Lao Tzu.*

Devas

1. The term "gods" is intended to refer to both male and female expressions of deity.
2. Bailey, *A Treatise on Cosmic Fire.*
3. Newton, *Journey of Souls Case Studies of Life between Lives.*
4. Bailey, *A Treatise on Cosmic Fire,* 913.
5. Ibid., 912.
6. Ibid.
7. Ibid.
8. Ibid., 646.
9. Ibid., 90.
8. Bailey, *Esoteric Healing,* 646–47.
9. Bailey, *A Treatise on Cosmic Fire,* 912.
10. Ibid., 53–54.
11. Ibid., 913.
12. Bailey, *Esoteric Healing,* 646–47.
13. Bailey, *A Treatise on Cosmic Fire,* 914.
14. For example, *Enochian Vision Magick* by Lon Milo DuQuette.
15. Bailey, *A Treatise on Cosmic Fire,* 466.
16. Ibid., 950–51.
17. This is discussed in *Esoteric Healing.*
18. Both Alice A. Bailey and Helena Blavatsky refer to the fallen angels in *A Treatise on Cosmic Fire* and *The Secret Doctrine,* respectively. See in particular page 1360 of *The Secret Doctrine* (Kindle edition).
19. Bailey, *A Treatise on Cosmic Fire,* 914, 66. See footnote 24 on page 66, which reads as follows: *Chohan (Tibetan). A Lord or Master. A high Adept. An initiate who has taken more initiations than the five major Initiations which make man a "Master of the Wisdom."*

Gods, Archangels, and Masters

1. Bailey, *A Treatise on Cosmic Fire*, 233–34.
2. Ibid., 677–78.

The Shadow People

1. (London: I. B. Taurus, 2014), 3.
2. (Scarlet Imprint, 2018), xiii.
3. Robert Lebling, *Legends of the Fire Spirits Jinn and Genies from Arabia to Zanzibar* (London: I. B. Taurus, 2010), 144–48.
4. Dr. Abu Ameenah Bilal Philips, *Ibn Taymiyah's Essay on the Jinn (Demons)* (Saudi Arabia: International Islamic Publishing House, 2007), 17.
5. Lebling, *Legends of the Fire Spirits Jinn and Genies from Arabia to Zanzibar*, 1–2.

Ghosts

1. Bailey, *Esoteric Healing*, 341.
2. Ibid., 487.
3. Bailey, *Esoteric Healing*, part 2, 380.

Supernatural Objects

1. Swords, which represent the element of air that correlates to the Divine Word, are often used in ritual magic and exorcisms.

5: DIVINITY

1. Lincoln, *Tao Te Ching—Lao Tzu*.
2. Blavatsky, *The Secret Doctrine*, 1705.
3. Ibid., 2605.

6: EVIL

1. Lincoln, *Tao Te Ching—Lao Tzu*.
2. In *Esoteric Astrology* (London: Lucis, 2017), Alice A. Bailey distinguishes between seven sacred planets and five nonsacred planets. Note that this system is not recognized by mainstream astrology, which does *not* mean that it is not valid. Readers are encouraged to explore this for themselves; information will be made available to them according to their own particular evolutionary requirements.
3. Bailey, *A Treatise on Cosmic Fire*, 214–16.
4. Ibid., 989–90.

7: THE CONSCIOUS UNIVERSE

1. Lincoln, *Tao Te Ching—Lao Tzu.*
2. For a deep dive into esoteric astrology, refer to Alice A. Bailey, *Esoteric Astrology* (London: Lucis, 2017).
3. An example of a triangular configuration between planets would be the evolutionary dualities that must play out between Earth (operating under the Law of Attraction) and other planets that are still operating purely within the paradigm of matter or form; conflict ensues until a third mediating planet intervenes to bring about balance between Spirit and matter.
4. Bailey, *Esoteric Astrology*, 506.
5. Ibid., 507.
6. Ibid., 54.
7. Ibid.
8. Ibid., 11.
9. *Esoteric Astrology* (London: Lucis, 2017).
10. Bailey, *A Treatise on Cosmic Fire*, 794.

8: JUDICIOUS AWAKENING

1. Jowlett, "Phaedo," in *Plato: Complete Works*, 12554–62
2. (London: Lucis, 2017)
3. Bailey, *A Treatise on Cosmic Fire*, 214–16.
4. Ibid., 46.
5. "Antahkarana" means "inner sense organ" in Sanskrit.
6. Bailey, *A Treatise on Cosmic Fire*, 123.
7. Ibid., 45–47.
8. Ibid., 126.
9. Ibid., 582.
10. Ibid., 127.
11. Ibid., 1126.
12. Ibid., 991–92.
13. Ibid., 490–91.
14. Ibid., 1126.
15. Ibid., 992.
16. Ibid.
17. Ibid., 615.
18. Dowsing crystals are used for divination; they typically comprise a triangular-shaped crystal attached to a short chain.

GLOSSARY

ajna chakra: The third-eye chakra

antahkarana: The so-called rainbow bridge that a person builds to access their higher faculties by connecting the personality to Divinity (or in the case of black magic, connecting the personality to devas on the mental planes rather than to Divinity); the "inner sense organ" in Sanskrit

astral body: The emotional or desire body; the seat of desires and emotions and the center of human beings' sentient responses (*see also* etheric body)

astral plane: An illusory state of consciousness created by humanity, born of excessive emotion and the desires of the personality (as distinct from the cocreative, intelligent desire implicit in the Law of Attraction)

asuras: In Hinduism (apart from in the oldest parts of the Rig Veda), evil beings. In Zoroastrianism, benevolent beings.

buddhic plane: The plane above the physical planes of humanity; the fourth ether

causal body: The higher mind; the ego; the higher elements of the nature of the human being

chakras: The seven major centers of energy formed by the intersection of lines of force within the etheric body

chi: Vital force or energy; prana

Council of Elders: A group of twelve highly evolved devas who previously incarnated as human beings and work alongside humanity in humanity's best interests

devas: In this book, a wide-ranging term to describe a class of entities of fundamental importance to human beings. In Hinduism, during the Vedic period, devas were divine beings (or deities) who were generally regarded as benevolent. In Zoroastrianism, devas were regarded as evil beings.

Divinity: The ineffable source of all things, transcending creation; the Source; the Logos

dharana: The Sanskrit concept of "concentration"

dharma: In Hinduism, cosmic law expressed by human beings as adherence to right behavior and social order

etheric body: The vital, astral, or emotional body. It receives, assimilates, and transmits life force from the sun to vitalize the body and separates the astral body from the gross physical body until the consciousness is sufficiently developed so as to be able to access other (nonphysical) planes.

etheric cord: Bridges the physical body and the etheric body and is part of the network of interlacing channels composing the etheric body. It magnetically links the physical body with its etheric double to the astral body, and to Divinity, through polarization.

etheric plane: The etheric state of consciousness; the ethers

green devas: Devas who protect the vegetable kingdom and those places on Earth in which energy vortices or magnetism occurs

guardian angel: A spirit guide; a higher being tasked with aiding one or more human beings from birth; a white deva

higher intelligence: Intelligence of the higher mind or guidance from an individual's spirit guides

higher mind: The causal body or ego; part of the soul; the higher elements of the nature of the human being

higher self: The mental body; the center of consciousness; the faculty that allows human beings to think

Ida: In the Hindu tradition, one of the three etheric channels housed in the spinal column; the other two are the Pingala and Sushumna channels. Associated with the parasympathetic nervous system and the right hemisphere of the brain.

kundalini: The "serpent power" situated at the base of the spine; an active or emanating fire that animates and vitalizes the physical body; the medium through which the personality is able to express itself on the physical plane

Logos: Divinity; the ineffable source of all things, transcending creation; the Source

lunar angels: Devas that govern the base lunar (or material) nature (the personality)

magic: Working with energies or other beings to bring about specified changes or results

manas: Thought; the stuff of mind; light energy. It carries the vibration of the cosmic mental plane.

mental body: The center of consciousness; that which allows human beings to think; the higher self

mental plane: Responsible for building and containing the physical plane; the basis of the concept of time; the mental state of consciousness

monad: Pure Spirit; Divinity

permanent atoms: Three focal points of energy within the causal body of the human being—the mental unit, the astral permanent atom, and the physical permanent atom, corresponding respectively to the lowest three levels of the solar system (the physical, emotional, and mental planes), together representing the cosmic physical plane

personality: Comprises the etheric (or vital, astral, or emotional) bodies, and the lower mind

physical body: The dense physical body together with the etheric body, both of which operate on the physical plane

physical plane: The physical state of consciousness

Pingala: In the Hindu tradition, one of the three etheric channels housed in the spinal column; the other two are the Ida and Sushumna channels. Associated with the sympathetic nervous system and the left hemisphere of the brain.

prana: Vital force or energy; chi

pranayama: Harnessing the breath through specific breathing exercises to circulate oxygen and prana around the body

sahasrara: The crown chakra

savasana: "Corpse" (Sanskrit) pose in the practice of yoga; the final resting pose necessary for the nervous system to assimilate the practice and for prana to be assimilated by the etheric body

solar angels: Devas that play an important role in the development of human beings' individuated or realized consciousness on the mental plane; they are integral to the spiritual (as opposed to physical) evolution of human beings, to whom they pass on their wisdom.

solar fire: The fires of mind; mental fire

soul: The combination of Spirit and matter; the self-conscious, thinking entity; the causal body or ego that persists through time and space; the principle of mind (the combination of lower and higher mind). It exists partly in the mental plane and attaches to the physical body in a subplane of the physical plane. It is composed of manas (or light energy) and expresses itself through (1) the individual souls of atoms making up the physical appearance, (2) the personality, and (3) the spirit, its higher aspect, which is connected to Divinity. The opposite number of the personality.

soul group: A group of familiar souls whom an individual encounters repeatedly in successive incarnations; the group tends to have common personal growth objectives.

Spirit: (1) Divinity; (2) the higher level or aspect of the human soul that is connected to Divinity; (3) a higher being such as a spirit guide that is also connected to Divinity

Spirit guide (guide): A higher being tasked with aiding one or more human beings by acting as a guardian from birth; a white deva

Sushumna: In the Hindu tradition, the central channel of the three etheric channels housed in the spinal column; the other two are the Ida and Pingala channels.

sutratma: The "silver thread" connecting the causal body with the physical brain at the beginning of a period of incarnation and withdrawing at the point of death. It connects the individual human being to Divinity via the causal vehicle. It functions as a permanent record of the individual's experiences throughout their lifetimes of incarnation and houses the permanent atoms.

violet devas: Devas who concern themselves with the "evolutionary development" of the etheric body. They also play a role in bolstering the astral body's defenses, grounding, and inspiring confidence and courage.

vishuddha chakra: The throat chakra

white devas: Guardian angels who are tasked with the day-to-day support of human beings